"Tara Edelschick and Kathy Tuan-MacLean unpack motherhood—in all its un-nerving, beautiful, transformative, exhausting, and confusing aspects—under the warm glow of gospel light. The truths are salient, practical, and delivered with a kind transparency that stands in stark contrast to the ways social media and the culture might afflict 'maternal norms' on women. If you feel inadequate raising your children, if you feel like a failure, if you feel like your kids deserve more than you have to offer, *Moms at the Well* is a balm of encouragement that can transform the way you see yourself, your family, and your loving God."

**Nancy French,** author, storyteller, and investigative journalist

"As I began to read *Moms at the Well*, I was hooked by the introduction! I teach a women's Bible study with lots of young mothers, and I look forward to gifting each of them with a copy of this book! Moms today experience a loneliness and a sense of helplessness that this delightfully honest book recognizes. Based on Scripture and made readable and interactive by design, this book reads like fresh water for thirsty moms!"

**Robbie Castleman,** author of *Parenting in the Pew*

"This wise and creative study offers a lifeline for less-than-perfect moms, for those who don't have it all together and struggle with self-doubt, anger, competition, invisibility, need for control, and the like. Tara Edelschick and Kathy Tuan-MacLean are vul-nerable and transparent, courageously sharing their own failures, heartaches, and fears regarding motherhood. Their study invites us to walk with biblical women who lived with circumstances they did not choose and with wounds they could not heal. Their lives become lenses that open our eyes to ourselves and to the God who comes to be with us. You will be thankful for *Moms at the Well*."

**Adele Ahlberg Calhoun,** author of the *Spiritual Disciplines Handbook* and *Spiritual Rhythms for the Enneagram*

"This book is a remarkable resource for moms, but its fundamental focus on spiritual formation is relevant for everyone. It illuminates how the loving hand of God can shape and refine us through the joys and challenges of parenting. Tara Edelschick and Kathy Tuan-MacLean invite us to drink deeply from the well of stories of mothers in the Bible, to reflect on the Holy Spirit's activity in our lives, and to practice spiritual exercises that deepen our connection with God."

**Tim and Joyce Dalrymple,** president and CEO of Christianity Today (Tim) and author and ministry leader (Joyce)

"*Moms at the Well* has wisdom that is tested in the world, refined by everyday real-life pressures, and crafted into this helpful resource. Thoughtfully and with reliable insights, the authors developed a study that truly meets parents in their deepest questions. The advice is simple and practical—dinnertime questions that help me connect my faith to my kids or applications of sabbath for different ages. The book works (judgment free) for busy parents navigating complicated time—I highly recommend *Moms at the Well*."

**Nikki Toyama-Szeto,** executive director of Christians for Social Action

"Maybe you love books written for moms. Maybe you usually don't like books written for moms. Maybe you often feel as if books for moms are written for some other kind of mom, not you. Whatever kind of mom you are—and even if rather than a mom, you're an aunt, dad, uncle, or friend—this book offers you a wealth of deep, honest engagement with stories from Scripture of ten people (some moms, some childless women, and even a dad) who encounter God's invitation to be transformed by his love."

**Catherine H. Crouch,** mom and professor of physics at Swarthmore College

"To more fully know God, we need community. To be better mothers to our children, we need community. My friends Tara Edelschick and Kathy Tuan-MacLean get that, and they want you to get that too. Their new insights into well-known Bible stories beautifully point us to God and encourage our hearts as we walk out being faithful, loving moms. Collect a group of moms you know—whatever their stage of life—and do this study. You will be grateful you did."

**Shaunti Feldhahn,** author of *For Women Only* and *Find Rest*

"*Moms at the Well* lives up to its name. Here we find cool, refreshing wisdom and encouragement for mothers everywhere. These devotions are richly researched, raw, and revelatory. They beckon us as moms to freshly encounter Christ, experience healing, and flourish right where we are."

**Michelle T. Sanchez,** author of *Color-Courageous Discipleship* and *God's Beloved Community*

"In *Moms at the Well*, Tara Edelschick and Kathy Tuan-MacLean offer an honest, practical, thoughtful, and life-seasoned study of mothers in the Bible who encounter God time and again in a process of persistent and patient spiritual transformation. The invitations to reflect on Scripture and personal experience, to engage in breath prayers, to check in with the Holy Spirit, and to practice family sabbath provide helpful ways to integrate this resource into a personal journey taken alongside others. This book will be much appreciated by mothers who need time at the well to be refreshed, renewed, and transformed."

**Maria Liu Wong,** provost of the City Seminary of New York and author of *On Becoming Wise Together: Learning and Leading in the City*

"I have had the privilege of learning from Tara Edelschick and Kathy Tuan-MacLean firsthand, witnessing how their tremendous wisdom flows out of more than two decades of deep community and rich spiritual practices. *Moms at the Well* is a rare gem that combines profound biblical insight, practical tools, and emotional depth. Best of all, it shows you how to engage the hard, holy work of parenting in community with others."

**Alison Cook,** therapist and author of *Boundaries for Your Soul: How to Turn Your Overwhelming Thoughts and Feelings into Your Greatest Allies*

# Moms *at the* Well

## MEETING GOD THROUGH THE
## MOTHERS OF SCRIPTURE

A **7-WEEK** BIBLE
STUDY EXPERIENCE

Tara Edelschick *and* Kathy Tuan-MacLean

IVP
Bible
Studies

An imprint of InterVarsity Press
Downers Grove, Illinois

**InterVarsity Press**
P.O. Box 1400 | Downers Grove, IL 60515-1426
ivpress.com | email@ivpress.com

InterVarsity Press® is the publishing division of InterVarsity Christian Fellowship/USA®. For more information, visit intervarsity.org.

All Scripture quotations, unless otherwise indicated, are taken from The Holy Bible, New International Version®, NIV®. Copyright © 1973, 1978, 1984, 2011 by Biblica, Inc.™ Used by permission of Zondervan. All rights reserved worldwide. www.zondervan.com. The "NIV" and "New International Version" are trademarks registered in the United States Patent and Trademark Office by Biblica, Inc.™

While any stories in this book are true, some names and identifying information may have been changed to protect the privacy of individuals.

Images on pages 54 and 109 appear courtesy of Kathy Tuan-MacLean. Used by permission.

Photos on pages 78 and 159 (Porch and Calligraphy) appear courtesy of Galen Zook and are used by permission.

Getty Images: winter scenery: 5279210107801613, cherry blossoms: Gollykim, lamb: Ata-Tur, chairs and tables: Jack N. Mohr, benches: 4Momentstoday, hands water: Pheelings Media, water bucket: Gary S Chapman, coffee cup: Skaman306, knitting: PixelsEffect, blue sofa: Predrag Popovski, café: Maryna Terletska, flower in vase: Alavinphoto, bread on table: Sebastian Rudnicki

"The Lanyard" from THE TROUBLE WITH POETRY: AND OTHER POEMS by Billy Collins, copyright © 2005 by Billy Collins. Used by permission of Random House, an imprint and division of Penguin Random House LLC. All rights reserved.

The publisher cannot verify the accuracy or functionality of website URLs used in this book beyond the date of publication.

Cover design: David Fassett
Interior design: Jeanna Wiggins
Images: Moment via Getty Images: © Nenov, © Carlina Teteris
iStock / Getty Images Plus: © Fototocam, © ajma_pl

ISBN 978-1-5140-0678-8 (print) | ISBN 978-1-5140-0679-5 (digital)

Printed in the United States of America ♾

**Library of Congress Cataloging-in-Publication Data**
A catalog record for this book is available from the Library of Congress.

29  28  27  26  25  24  |  8  7  6  5  4  3  2  1

# Contents

# Introduction

**We always wanted to be mothers,** yet neither of us was sure it would ever happen. For Kathy, it was because she was the "unmarriageable" daughter. For Tara, it was because her first baby was stillborn. So when God gave us children, we were delighted and grateful. As women with doctorates in human development, we thought we were going to be great mothers, mothers who didn't exhibit the sin patterns of our mothers and grandmothers, mothers who didn't yell or criticize or worry, mothers who would write the book on how to be great moms.

And then . . .

Motherhood hit.

If you saw us in our worst moments, you would agree that we are not the women to write about how to be great moms. Motherhood has been one of the most challenging experiences we've faced. Kathy calls the fourteen years of parenting three young children her "dark night of the soul." Tara's children say she has "dictator syndrome," often when she is struggling to believe that God is trustworthy to care for her children. Motherhood has stripped us bare, exposing our deepest fears and failures. Yet God has also used motherhood to transform our lives. In the midst of all of motherhood's highs and lows, Jesus invited us on a journey of spiritual transformation, deeper and deeper into his transforming love.

This Bible study, therefore, is not filled with advice on how to be a better mother. There are a ton of great books out there to help you do that; this just isn't one of them. Instead, by studying the lives of biblical women, especially mothers, we will meet the God who invites us into a process of spiritual transformation that takes place in five steps:

1. *God meets us where we are.*

2. *God welcomes us into honest conversation.*

3. *God calls us to trust and obey.*

4. *God transforms us and sets us free.*

5. *God invites us to be agents of shalom.*

What do you notice about these five steps? That's right—they all start with God. As we'll discover, God meets us where we are and then initiates every step along the way, allowing us to say yes or no to each invitation. While these steps are not necessarily linear—after all, God is never constrained by a formula—we've been surprised by how often they show up in the stories we read in Scripture, as well as in our own lives and experiences.

If you, like some of the women we will study, aren't always sure that God is good and can be trusted, that's okay. Getting to know God and God's character is what this Bible study series is all about. While God's love can feel more tangible when life is sweet, these studies help us experience God's good news for us when we feel afraid, angry, envious, or just plain miserable.

Motherhood gives us the chance to experience God's transformative love in the midst of both the highs and the lows. Jesus will be there through the joy of wobbly first steps, the warmth of cuddles, and the pride of watching your child accomplish something she never thought she could. And he will be there through sleepless nights and temper tantrums, anxious days waiting for a scary diagnosis, angry fights when your teen breaks curfew, and anguish as your adult child's marriage struggles. Jesus promises his transformational presence and love in the midst of it all.

What a great promise! Not only for us as individuals, but for our children, our communities, and our world. As God's love transforms our individual lives, we become agents of God's kingdom, joining God's mission of shalom—the biblical vision of harmony and wholeness for the whole world.

## YOU ARE NOT ALONE

We surveyed over seven hundred moms to better understand their experiences of motherhood and how those experiences affected their faith. These moms ranged in age from twenty-three to more than sixty years old, and had anywhere from one to seven children. Twenty-four percent of them were single, adoptive, divorced, or fostering parents; nearly 40 percent were women of color. To better understand our survey results, we conducted in-depth interviews with more than a dozen women. Each of their stories was unique, shaped by their personalities and histories, and each was inspirational. And yet each

**WHEN ASKED TO DESCRIBE THE HARDEST PARTS OF PARENTING, THE MOST COMMON RESPONSES SOUND LIKE THOSE FROM THESE EIGHT RESPONDENTS:**

1. I don't have other mothers with whom I can share what's really going on with me and my family. It's lonely.

2. I used to be so close to God. But after children, I don't have time to do what I used to do.

3. The amount of worry I have for my children can take my breath away.

4. The gospel that is preached is too thin to help me navigate my experience of motherhood.

5. I never know if God thinks I am being too lenient or too strict, working too much or too little, etc.

6. I can't balance it all, and I feel like I am failing at everything.

7. I have so little control over my temper, my children's decisions, and their safety—and I feel vulnerable.

8. I see my own sin in my children and I feel hopeless to change it.

of them, along with our survey respondents, expressed different ways that motherhood was difficult, really difficult.

From our surveys and interviews, we learned that moms struggle with worry, escapism, comparison, anger, a desire for control, and even feelings of heartbreak. Perhaps not surprising, moms found it difficult to connect with God amid these struggles. They couldn't find time to pray or read the Bible. Many felt hopeless about some aspect of parenting, and some even said they found parenting so difficult it caused them to doubt the existence of God. The women in our survey expressed a longing to experience God's transformational love in the midst of some really tough stuff.

Maybe you share that longing as well. If so, you are not alone, and these studies are for you.

## MEETING AT THE WELL

Because loneliness in mothering was reported by the majority of the women who took our survey, we've designed the studies in this book to be enjoyed with a friend or small group. We think of the studies as a way for moms to gather at the well.

In ancient times (and in many places in the world today) women spent large parts of their day at wells, drawing water for their families. They needed water for drinking, cleaning, and watering their animals and crops. Getting this life-saving water took work. Wells were usually located outside of town: every morning women walked the path to the well, balancing a large clay jar on their head or shoulders. They drew water from the deep well, then carried the even heavier jar home. But the difficult work had its upsides; it provided a social time as friends and neighbors walked together, took turns drawing water, and enjoyed each other's company.

We have our own wells, places where moms gather regularly: at playgroups and playgrounds; on sidelines and in bleachers; in break rooms and waiting rooms; at band concerts and PTA fundraisers; and in our living rooms and church basements for Bible study and prayer. When these "wells" are healthy, we are seen and heard, encouraged and challenged. We find the water we need to get us and our families through the next day.

These wells are also great places to meet God. This shouldn't surprise us: God was always meeting women at wells. The Bible uses several different words to describe places to get water; *wells*, *springs*, and *fountains* are present from Genesis to Revelation, and God shows up at them all. God found Hagar at a well when she fled abuse. God orchestrated Rebekah's marriage to Isaac when she came to draw water from a well. And Jesus waited for the Samaritan woman at a well. Whether our biblical sisters were fleeing abuse, taking care of their families, or hiding from their scornful neighbors, God met them where they were. Women spent much of their day at wells—ordinary days, painful days, and even days of crisis. So naturally God showed up at wells.

Think of this book as a way to gather with other mothers at a well and drink in God's life-sustaining water. Each study is designed to be practical and user friendly for busy and tired moms, and each includes several sections: a video with important biblical background, a group study, five daily devotionals, and a sabbath activity to enjoy with your whole family.

As you work through each study, we encourage you to notice where the Holy Spirit nudges you to pause, listen, and pray. Many of us are tempted to think, talk, and problem solve, rather than ask God for insight and help. To help you stop and listen, reflection sections often include an invitation to pause and ask the Holy Spirit to speak to you. As you do, we think you'll be surprised by how consistently God shows up—revealing truth and showering you with love and grace.

Whether it takes you seven weeks or seven years to walk with God through these studies, we pray that you will be richly blessed. As you gather at the well and dig into God's Word, may you experience Jesus drawing near, inviting you on a journey of spiritual transformation. We urge you to accept his invitation and follow him. We have, and it's changed everything.

## GROUP COMMITMENTS

Groups function well when members share the same commitments about how to interact. Look at these suggested commitments, and decide if your group would like to keep, modify, or add any.

1. Listen actively without giving advice
2. Let folks finish their thoughts without interrupting
3. Take wise risks to share the vulnerable truth about your life
4. Be mindful of how much space you take up in the group (if you're a talker, listen more; if you're a listener, talk a little more)
5. Have a learning posture
6. Be open to what God has for you
7. Keep confidentiality—what's said in the group stays in the group

# When We Feel Unseen

## GROUP BIBLE STUDY

### INTRODUCTION TO WEEK 1

Have someone read the following aloud:

It's easy to feel unseen as a mom. We feel unseen when no one appreciates the countless dinners, playdates, and appointments we've made happen. We feel unseen when we get no credit for the never-ending to-do list we carry in our heads, trying to keep every living being in the house fed, clothed, and somewhat in their right minds. We feel unseen when our real lives, with our real hopes and struggles, aren't reflected in family leave policies, social media trends, or even in the sermons we hear each week. In a culture that renders the real lives of mothers invisible, the story of Hagar gives us great hope. An enslaved Egyptian outsider, Hagar is seen only as a potentially fertile servant. Her enslavers never even call her by name. Yet God sees Hagar, and God sees each of us. God meets Hagar at a well and is waiting to meet us too.

### OPENING ACTIVITY

READ aloud this poem by Billy Collins.

**"The Lanyard"**
The other day I was ricocheting slowly
off the blue walls of this room,
moving as if underwater from typewriter to piano,
from bookshelf to an envelope lying on the floor,
when I found myself in the L section of the dictionary
where my eyes fell upon the word lanyard.

No cookie nibbled by a French novelist
could send one into the past more suddenly—
a past where I sat at a workbench at a camp
by a deep Adirondack lake
learning how to braid long thin plastic strips
into a lanyard, a gift for my mother.

I had never seen anyone use a lanyard
or wear one, if that's what you did with them,
but that did not keep me from crossing
strand over strand again and again
until I had made a boxy
red and white lanyard for my mother.

She gave me life and milk from her breasts,
and I gave her a lanyard.
She nursed me in many a sick room,
lifted spoons of medicine to my lips,
laid cold face-cloths on my forehead,
and then led me out into the airy light

and taught me to walk and swim,
and I, in turn, presented her with a lanyard.
Here are thousands of meals, she said,
and here is clothing and a good education.
And here is your lanyard, I replied,
which I made with a little help from a counselor.

Here is a breathing body and a beating heart,
strong legs, bones and teeth,
and two clear eyes to read the world, she whispered,
and here, I said, is the lanyard I made at camp.
And here, I wish to say to her now,
is a smaller gift—not the worn truth

that you can never repay your mother,
but the rueful admission that when she took
the two-tone lanyard from my hand,
I was as sure as a boy could be
that this useless, worthless thing I wove
out of boredom would be enough to make us even

**SHARE:** When you think back about your own mother (or another person who raised you), what do you appreciate about them now that you didn't see at the time?

**VIDEO**
**WATCH** this week's video.

**BIBLE STUDY**
**READ** Genesis 16 aloud.

1. How do Abram and Sarai treat Hagar and refer to her in verses 1-6?

2. Why do you think Hagar despises Sarai?

3. What challenges might Hagar face making the 210-mile journey to Shur? How likely is it that she will survive?

4. When the angel meets Hagar near the well in the desert in verse 7, how do you imagine she is doing:
   - physically?

   - emotionally?

   - spiritually?

5. Imagining the labels others might have used to describe Hagar—foreigner, runaway, slave—what might it have meant to her that the angel of the Lord called her by name in verse 8?

6. How are the two questions in verse 8 an invitation for Hagar to have an honest conversation with God? How does she respond?

7. What does God tell Hagar to do in verse 9? Why would it be difficult to obey?

8. Identify the prophecies made in each verse:

   – verse 10

   – verse 11

   – verse 12 (note: a wild donkey is akin to a wild mustang, roaming the plains freely)

9. How could these prophecies make it easier for Hagar to obey the angel's difficult command?

10. In verse 13, Hagar gives God the name "You are the God who sees me." Out of all the names Hagar could have given God, why do you think she chose this one?

11. Later in Scripture, God fulfills all of the angel's prophecies, including that Ishmael will be free. But there are small signs of transformation even in this story.

   — Beer Lahai Roi means the well of the Living One who sees me. What needed to happen for the well to have this name hundreds of years after the angel meets Hagar there (v. 14)?

   — Why is it significant that Abram named his son Ishmael (v. 15)?

# Holy Spirit Check-In

Your Christian tradition may not emphasize listening to the Holy Spirit. But Scripture tells us that the Holy Spirit comforts, guides, teaches, instructs, convicts, helps, and intercedes for us. Not only that, the Spirit speaks to us (John 16:13-14)! If you are new to listening to the Holy Spirit, these studies give you plenty of opportunities to experiment, often with a one- or two-minute exercise. Rarely will you hear an audible voice. Instead, the Spirit may speak through a thought, a picture, a Scripture, or an impression. We have been amazed at how much the Spirit can do if we are willing to spend even a minute listening.

# Breath Prayer

Breath prayer is a simple ancient practice that helps us pray throughout the day using our breath as a guide. We can use breath prayer as we walk, as we grocery shop, or during pauses at work. Breath prayer is great for busy moms—we simply breathe in a short phrase and breathe out another one.

## HOLY SPIRIT CHECK-IN

Take one minute to tell the Holy Spirit about places you feel unseen or unheard. Then listen for one minute to hear what the Holy Spirit says in response. Briefly share what you experienced.

## BREATH PRAYER

Take two minutes of silence to practice this breath prayer individually. Then share what, if anything, you experienced while praying. If you feel drawn to this prayer, you can practice it throughout the week.

> INHALE: *God who sees me*
>
> EXHALE: *See me now*

## LEADER BENEDICTION

*El Roi, thank you that you are the God who sees us. Thank you that you are the God who hears us. We long to meet you, to have genuine honest conversation with you. Yet we confess that it's often hard to tell you the truth about where we are right now. We either don't believe you'll speak to us, or we don't stop to hear your voice. We want to trust you, to obey you, to experience your transforming love, and to partner with you as an agent of shalom in the world. Help us to say yes to your invitations. Amen.*

## GOD MEETS HAGAR WHERE SHE IS

*Day 1*

When our story begins, the family that has enslaved Hagar sees her as property, good for serving her mistress and bearing her owners a child. She may have heard them talk about their God, the God who promised them a great legacy. But for Hagar, Abram's God is the god of her enslavers, a god who allowed the circumstances that brought her to slavery, who gives her no choices about where she lives, who she works for, who she has sex with, who impregnates her, and who takes her child.

> **REFLECT:** *In Genesis 16:1-6, given how Hagar's been treated by Abram and Sarai, what do you think she felt about the god of her enslavers?*

This dysfunctional family of God lives in a cycle of pain and abuse. Hagar, pregnant with Abram's child, despises Sarai. Sarai blames Abram for the consequences of her plan. Abram disengages, saying, "Your slave is in your hands. . . . Do with her whatever you think best." He's a bystander who enables unjust treatment. Sarai mistreats Hagar so badly that Hagar takes off alone into the desert, heading back to Egypt despite the odds that she likely won't survive the journey. If she does survive, there may be no family with the means to support her and her child when she gets there.

Hagar is alone, vulnerable, and unseen.

> **OBSERVE** *Genesis 16:7-8: Identify everything the angel of the Lord does.*

This is the first time the angel of the Lord appears in Scripture, and he goes looking for Hagar until he finds her at a well. Think about that: the angel of the Lord comes to meet Hagar, one of the most marginalized people in Scripture—female, pregnant, enslaved, and sexually exploited. God comes to meet her where she is—alone, despised, and desperate.

The angel speaks to Hagar, calling her by name. Until this moment in the story, no one else has called her by her name, Hagar, which means *flight* or *forsaken*. We don't know who named her or why. Perhaps her parents, knowing they had to sell her into slavery, named her *flight* to express their hopes for her, or *forsaken* as they gave her up. But God knows her name and calls her by name, "Hagar."

The angel then calls Hagar by circumstance: "slave of Sarai." By recognizing her circumstance, God lets Hagar know that her desperate situation matters to God. The first step in the remarkable relationship between God and Hagar is that the angel comes to her in the midst of a crisis that he names but does not let define her.

Scripture gives us story after story of our good God pursuing people, whatever their name and whatever their situation. In fact, any spiritual impulse we have toward God happens because God takes the first step toward us. In Luke 15, Jesus describes himself as the shepherd who goes after lost sheep; the woman who relentlessly searches for her lost coin; the prodigal father who runs to welcome one lost son and then pleads for his other lost son to come into the party. Without insisting we reciprocate, God comes to us, always and everywhere. We don't have to earn God's presence; God goes looking and finds us wherever we are on our journey.

As with Hagar, God knows your name and your story. God knows where you've come from and where you're headed. God meets you wherever you are.

## GOD MEETS US WHERE WE ARE

How has God come to find you in the past? If you are unsure, try to identify experiences where God sought you through:

— friends, family, or coworkers

— an experience in nature

— prayer, Bible study, or worship

— signs, wonders, or dreams

If you can't identify anything yet, don't worry. Learning to see God's hand in your life is part of the journey of spiritual transformation.

## GOD WELCOMES HAGAR AND SARAI INTO HONEST CONVERSATION

*Day 2*

Throughout Scripture, rather than lecturing, preaching, or ranting about what we've done wrong, God often greets us with questions, inviting us into a conversation. In Genesis 16:8, God calls out to Hagar and asks two questions at the heart of spiritual transformation:

*Where have you come from?*

*Where are you going?*

> **REFLECT:** *How might these questions have made Hagar feel? How might she have been tempted to lie?*

Hagar answers the first question—she is running away from her mistress. It's astounding that Hagar told the angel the truth when she had little reason to believe that God cared about her. Maybe the way God called her by name, or looked her in the eye and smiled at her, gave her the courage. Hagar doesn't answer the second question, though—perhaps because she doesn't know where she's going. She doesn't know if she'll survive the journey. She doesn't know whether her family will receive her in Egypt. She doesn't know what will become of her child. Perhaps she hasn't even let herself hope for a better future but is simply desperate to get away from her abusive past.

Even though God already knows the answers, God asks questions because they invite us into relationship. God wants to hear what we have to say, and then respond. Back and forth, back and forth, until we're talking with God like a friend.

Questions aren't the only way God initiates conversations with us, but they are gifts each time they arise. They help us discern what's going on in our lives and help us know what God thinks we should focus on. If you're not sure about how powerful questions are, read through the Gospels and note the three-hundred-plus questions Jesus asks. Imagine what might change in your relationship with God if you read those questions as Jesus welcoming you into conversation, spent time wrestling with those questions, and asked Jesus questions of your own. Though some of us were raised to believe questioning is unspiritual, wrestling with questions—both God's and ours—actually deepens our relationship with God.

Even though God welcomes us into conversation, talking with God isn't always easy. When our story is painful, we may have a hard time talking honestly with God because it's too hard to face the pain. Other times, we feel ashamed and sharing leaves us feeling vulnerable. God never demands that we share. We have the power to spurn God's invitation, and this is what happens with Sarah in Genesis 18.

For thirteen years, Sarah's heard her husband, Hagar, and all the people of her camp call out "Ishmael" over and over—thirteen years of being told that "God hears" and wondering if God hears everyone but her. Now ninety, she overhears Abraham talking with three angels who promise, yet again, that Abraham will have a child through her.

**OBSERVE** *Genesis 18:10-15: What does Sarah say as she laughs? What do you think this reveals about her thoughts, hopes, and faith?*

Despite Abraham having regular conversations with God throughout his life, this is the only place where we see Sarah have that opportunity. Eavesdropping at the entrance to the tent, hearing the men talk about her deepest hopes, Sarah laughs to herself and doubts the visitors' promise. But God sees Sarah and hears what's on her heart even when she's hidden from plain view. God wants to start an honest conversation with her, inviting her in by asking Abraham why Sarah laughed. Sarah joins the conversation, but she is afraid and lies.

Laughing in response to God's impossible promise isn't a deal breaker—Abraham did it a chapter earlier and God didn't hold it against him; they just kept on talking. So why is Sarah afraid? Maybe it hurts too much to face her identity as "barren" again. Perhaps she can't get her hopes up one more time only to be crushed by disappointment. Or maybe she is simply afraid to tell God that she laughed because she doesn't trust that God cares about her or her dreams. Whatever caused her fear, when invited by God to share the truth, Sarah lies.

And the conversation stops right there.

Too often, like Sarah, we short-circuit our intimacy with God because we are afraid or unwilling to tell God the truth about where we are. The good news is that God is constantly waiting and eager to begin the conversation.

# GOD WELCOMES US INTO HONEST CONVERSATION

1. Right this moment, without thinking too deeply about it, how do you respond to the angel's questions to Hagar:

   *Where have you come from?*

   *Where are you going?*

2. In what areas of your life have you stopped the conversation with God? Why?

**AN INVITATION: HOLY SPIRIT PAUSE**

Make a note card with the two questions the angel first asks Hagar: *Where have you come from? Where are you going?* Leave the card somewhere where you often find yourself rushing, like the dashboard of your car or the laundry room. When you see the card, take one deep breath and then share your answer with the Holy Spirit. It need not be deep. Your answer may be, "I just left an important work meeting. I'm headed to pick up the kids." Or it may sound more like,

"I just left two children fighting in the living room. I'm trying to get a load of laundry done before I start dinner." After sharing your answers, take a deep breath in, hold it for the count of five, then breathe out, "You see me, you hear me, God."

## GOD CALLS HAGAR TO TRUST AND OBEY

Day 3

Hagar takes the risk of telling God the truth. And for a time, it isn't clear that telling the truth is the right idea—because God tells her to go back and submit to Sarai.

Why would God tell Hagar to go back and submit to her mistress, to return to oppression and mistreatment? Everything feels wrong about that command. After all, nothing has changed. Hagar will continue to be enslaved. As far as she knows, her son will belong to another woman. Hagar will still be a foreigner, a slave, a powerless outsider exploited at the whims of the family insiders. Nothing has changed.

And yet everything has changed.

> **REFLECT** *on Genesis 16:9-12: How would naming her son Ishmael, "God hears," help Hagar trust and obey God's command to go back to slavery?*

Hagar enters the desert with no hope and no future. She leaves with hope and a destiny. She now has a relationship with the God who has seen and heard her misery, a God who gives her a set of promises, including that she will have descendants too numerous to count— almost identical to the promise God gave Abram in chapter fifteen.

In the middle of the list of promises, God says that Ishmael will be a "wild donkey of a man." Reading this today, that doesn't sound like a compliment; but in Hagar's ancient world, wild donkeys were free—more akin to wild mustangs. God promises Hagar that her son will not be enslaved and will father a free and nomadic nation. In other words, God doesn't ask Hagar to accept slavery, but to trust that someday her son will be free.

God invites Hagar to trust that even if she's unseen in Sarai's family, *God sees her*. Even if Abram never hears her cries of misery, *God hears her*. She is the woman who has seen God face-to-face. Her son and his freedom will evidence God's great love for Hagar. While her circumstances have not yet changed, her identity has. She is the one who is seen, heard, and loved by God.

> **REFLECT:** *So many promises in the Bible will not be fulfilled right away, or even in this lifetime. How does knowing that God sees, hears, and loves you make it easier for you to trust God during times of suffering and waiting for God's promises to be fulfilled?*

Hagar gives God the name *El Roi*, which can be translated, "The God who sees me." Hagar is the first and only person in all of Scripture who dares name God. She obeys God's very difficult command to return to Sarai because she's met a good God who sees her and hears her cries, a good God who promises a great future for her son. God's promises bring much better news than what awaits her alone in the desert. So she obeys the angel and returns.

Some people struggle with the word *obey*. To modern ears, obedience can sound oppressive. But obeying God simply means doing what God wants, trusting that God's love and intentions for us are so good that we would be foolish not to obey.

As with Hagar, God sometimes speaks to us directly and clearly, guiding our steps on a specific path. Usually, though, God's hardest commandments are already in Scripture: love your enemies, pray for those who persecute you, give generously, do justice, love mercy, and walk humbly with your God. Yet every one of these difficult commands brings another opportunity to trust and obey. Transformation happens when we, like Hagar, trust in God's goodness and obey God's commands.

## GOD CALLS US TO TRUST AND OBEY

1. Where do you find it easy to trust God? Where do you find it difficult?

2. How do you respond to the word *obey*? How might knowing that God is El Roi, the One who sees, make it easier?

**AN INVITATION: HOLY SPIRIT PAUSE**

Trust and obedience are like muscles that get stronger as you exercise them. Ask the Holy Spirit to show you one place you could trust God, and one baby step of obedience you could take today. Write it down, try it, and notice what happens.

# GOD TRANSFORMS HAGAR AND SETS HER FREE

We don't know specifics about Hagar's relationship with El Roi after she returns to camp. Did her encounter with El Roi change how she interacts with Sarai and Abram? Did it change her vision of the community she lives in? How might she now see others who are marginalized or victimized like herself?

> **REFLECT:** *Take a minute to imagine how Hagar, knowing the God who both sees and hears her, now relates to those who enslave her. How do you think her interactions with Sarai and Abram might differ from earlier interactions?*

We won't know Hagar's full story this side of heaven. But the story reveals some astonishing transformations: Sarai does not adopt Ishmael as she had originally intended, so Hagar gets to keep her son; because Hagar returns to camp, Ishmael grows up with his father; and Abraham, so uncaring he allowed the mother of his unborn child to suffer terribly, grows to love Ishmael. In chapter 17, when Abraham learns that God's covenant will be fulfilled through Sarah's child, he begs God for Ishmael to live under God's blessing as well.

> **OBSERVE** *Genesis 17:15-21: How does God respond to Abraham's request that Ishmael live under God's blessing? What are the promises God gives about Ishmael?*

Hagar's difficult decision to trust and obey God puts her and her son in a place where God can care for and bless them until they are free. That freedom is many years down the road, but even when freedom is incomplete, God is at work.

God is always inviting us into a process of transformation. Our role is to say yes. We say yes when we tell God the truth about our stories. We say yes when we trust God with our future and our children's futures. We say yes when we obey God's commands. God does not transform us against our will; God honors our no. But when we, like Hagar, say yes, God always begins the work of transformation and setting us free.

# GOD TRANSFORMS US AND SETS US FREE

1. Where have you said yes to God and experienced transformation?

2. Where might you have said no to God and short-circuited transformation?

## AN INVITATION: SAYING SORRY AND YES

Take a minute to tell God you're sorry for any times you said no in the past and ask for the courage and faith to say yes in the future. Write down anything you hear from God.

# GOD INVITES HAGAR TO
# BE AN AGENT OF SHALOM

*Day 5*

Shalom is God's vision of harmony, wholeness, and peace for all of creation—so important that it's mentioned 550 times in Scripture. In God's shalom, all is good and right within and between God's people and God's creation, and everyone has what they need to flourish.

God's kingdom is a kingdom of shalom. When Jesus announces that the kingdom of God is at hand (Mark 1:15), he ushers in a new reign of shalom—where he is restoring every part of creation, including us. The first four steps of spiritual transformation are all about our restoration. In the fifth step, having showered us with so much shalom, God invites us to pour that shalom into a world thirsty for good news. We are blessed to be a blessing.

After Hagar experiences shalom with God, she then becomes an agent of shalom for others, specifically her family that has treated her so badly. Imagine their surprise when Hagar returns and tells them about meeting the angel of the Lord— their God, not hers. Remarkably, Abram and his family believe Hagar's account of meeting El Roi. Perhaps, like Moses after seeing God face-to-face (Exodus 34), Hagar returns to camp with a face so radiant that her family listens to her.

> The Hebrew word *shalom* means harmony, wholeness, peace, prosperity, and welfare for all individuals and communities. When shalom abounds, God's people have what they need to flourish, and live out their purpose in the world—to love God, love neighbor, and steward creation together.

How do we know they received her witness as true? (1) Abram names their son Ishmael, the name God commanded (Genesis 16:14-16). (2) The family recognizes the importance of Hagar's encounter at the well and calls it *Beer Lahai Roi*, which means "well of the Living One who sees me," for centuries to come.

Because of Hagar's witness, Abram and his whole family discover more about the character of the God they follow. Through her witness, they learn that their God is a God who sees and hears—even pregnant, runaway slaves.

The greatest beneficiary of Hagar's shalom-bearing, though, is her son Ishmael.

Because Hagar says yes to God's invitations, Ishmael experiences more and more of God's vision for harmony and wholeness. He receives love from both his earthly father Abraham and his heavenly Father God. As a free man, Ishmael experiences the fulfillment of the angel's promise to Hagar in Genesis 16.

Hagar's faithfulness and witness allow her family to taste a little more of God's goodness.

Hagar's story gives us some hints of what shalom might look like for real moms raising real kids: *a little more shalom*. Clearly, Hagar and her son do not experience complete shalom. They spend many years enslaved. And as we'll read in week seven, Sarah convinces Abraham to exile Hagar and Ishmael into the desert. Hagar's faithfulness ushered in a *little more*—yet incomplete—*shalom*.

> **REFLECT:** *As you ponder the powerful yet incomplete shalom Hagar and her family experienced, do you feel encouraged, disheartened, or something else? Why?*

Just as it was for Hagar, the shalom we experience this side of heaven will always be fractured. We may struggle to believe we can be part of God's restoration of the world. Heck, we can scarcely get through an afternoon without exploding diapers, homework meltdowns, or moments hiding in the laundry room with a secret stash of last year's Halloween candy. How can we bring about the wholeness and well-being of our neighbors when there are days we can barely get dinner on the table before bedtime? Yet each of us is invited to taste the goodness of God and share that goodness with our families and neighbors. We can all bring just a little more shalom.

A little more shalom may look like apologizing to our teen for losing our tempers or seeking therapy so we don't transmit our pain to others. It might look like leaving dirty kids in our dirty house to bring a bag of groceries to a neighbor. Or reminding a friend whose infant cries all the time that you think she is doing a great job and praying that she would hear the same from God.

Hagar never witnessed the full legacy of the shalom she bore. She didn't know that the name she gave God would be written down or that her story would encourage countless women for generations to come. When we, like Hagar, go to the well of the Living One who sees us, we too can become imperfect agents of shalom in an imperfect world thirsty for harmony, wholeness, and peace.

## GOD INVITES US TO BE AGENTS OF SHALOM

1. When did you need "a little more shalom" during your day yesterday or today? What might a little more shalom have looked like?

2. As you imagine yourself experiencing more of God's shalom, how would you like to see it ripple out from you to your family, friends, or community?

## AN INVITATION: A LITTLE MORE SHALOM

Ask God to bring to mind a fellow mom who might need a little more shalom today. Write down her name and pray for her.

Send a short text or email letting her know that you see her and are praying for her. If you are feeling extra ambitious, you might invite her for coffee or send along a verse that would encourage her.

*Family Sabbath*

For those who may be new to sabbath, it is a day set aside each week to experience the fullness of God's shalom. Many families attend church, rest, and delight in God's creation. Because it can be hard to rest and delight when you are raising young children, each chapter suggests a simple way to experience God's goodness as a family. Rather than berating yourself for all the ways you think you are falling short on keeping the sabbath, you might embrace this one small moment of God's shalom with your family.

One of the greatest gifts we can give to our children is the gift of seeing them and hearing them. This week, take time at a meal to "see" and "hear" each other. You might start by saying:

*This week, I read a story in the Bible about a woman named Hagar. From her, I learned that God delights in us. That means that it makes God happy to see us and hear us. When we enjoy seeing and hearing each other, just like God saw and heard Hagar, we reflect God's love.*

Next, give each family member a chance to affirm one another with an "I saw" or "I heard" statement. Try either of the following.

1. "I saw . . .

   — your kind heart at the park yesterday."

   — how well you listened to your brother tell us about the game."

   — how your face lit up when you ate that ice cream."

   — you working really hard on your math unit even when you found it difficult."

Followed by: "I love seeing you."

2. "I heard . . .

   — you playing basketball in the driveway for hours."

   — you laughing with your friends on the phone."

   — you singing in the shower."

   — you asking politely for your sister to share the toy."

   — the worry in your voice when you talked about going to camp."

Followed by: "I love hearing you."

This is an easy activity to do if you are sharing a sabbath meal or snack with others.

## When We're Worried

# GROUP BIBLE STUDY

### CHECK IN ON LAST WEEK

Allow each person one to two minutes to share:

- How did your devotionals and family sabbath practice go last week? (No shame or guilt if you didn't get to them.)

- What did you hear (if anything) from God through the studies, the reflection questions, and the invitations?

### INTRODUCTION TO WEEK 2

Have someone read the following aloud:

Moms are worried and anxious about many things. Jesus knows that and encourages us to have faith in him. Mark 5 illustrates what faith might look like in the midst of fear through the stories of two daughters: a twelve-year-old who is dying and a woman who has bled for twelve years.

(Note: Because Jesus calls the bleeding woman "daughter," we name her *Batya*, which means "daughter of God" in Hebrew. Jesus calls the twelve-year-old *Talitha*, Aramaic for "little girl," so we will too. And we will refer to Talitha's mother as *Charis*, which is Greek for "grace.")

### OPENING ACTIVITY

VIDEO

WATCH this week's video.

A word cloud is a cluster of words displayed in a variety of sizes, colors, or shading. Larger, bolder words are those that are more important. Make a word cloud with words that describe the fears you have for your kids. Make the words big or small based on how much they resonate with your experience.

SHARE your word cloud with the group.

## BIBLE STUDY

READ Mark 5:21-43 aloud.

1. Compare and contrast Jairus and Batya.

COMPARING JAIRUS AND BATYA IN MARK 5

|  | JAIRUS | BATYA |
|---|---|---|
| Their social status | v. 22 | vv. 25-26 |
| The nature of their problem | v. 23 | vv. 25-26 |
| How they approach Jesus | vv. 21-24 | vv. 27-28 |
| What they fear | vv. 23, 35, 36 | v. 33 |

1. Why do you think Jesus, while dealing with a crisis, stopped to ask, "Who touched my clothes?" (v. 30). How did Batya feel at that moment? How did Jairus feel?

2. Jesus hears Batya's "whole truth" (v. 33). What details might she have talked about?

3. Jesus tells Batya her faith has made her well (v. 34). How has Batya shown faith?

4. What do you think Jairus thought or felt while listening to Batya's whole truth?

5. Before Jesus gets to Jairus's house, they receive the news that Talitha has died (vv. 35-36). What does Jesus ask Jairus to have faith in? What does faith look like for Jairus?

6. What do you imagine Charis, Jairus's wife, experiences as she waits for Jairus to return? As Talitha dies? When Jesus shows up and says Talitha is sleeping (v. 39)?

## HOLY SPIRIT CHECK-IN

We all experience dying in some way—if not physical death, then perhaps a dream or relationship is dying in your or your child's life. Take two minutes to ask the Holy Spirit to help you fill in the blanks:

*Jesus, _____ is dying, please come*

*and put your hands on _____ so*

*that _____ will be healed and live.*

**TAKE TURNS PRAYING** your prayer aloud.

## BREATH PRAYER

Take two minutes of silence to practice this breath prayer individually. Then share what, if anything, you experienced while praying. If you feel drawn to this prayer, you can pray it throughout the week.

**INHALE:** *I am afraid*

**EXHALE:** *Please come*

*Jesus, we worry about so many things. We want to trust you when you tell us "Do not worry." And yet, we still worry. About chronic problems and crises. About our own health and well-being and that of our children. Help us push through the crowds to be with you. Help us bring you home, even when it seems as though all hope is lost. Let us experience the peace of being in your presence, a peace that passes all understanding. Amen.*

## JESUS MEETS JAIRUS AND BATYA WHERE THEY ARE

*Day 1*

Imagine the scene in Mark 5:21-43. Jesus arrives in town by boat. As a large crowd presses around him by the lake, Jairus, a synagogue leader, breaks through, falls at his feet, and begs Jesus to come with him to heal his daughter. It's a medical crisis for a high-powered family.

> **REFLECT:** *Put yourself in the sandals of Jairus and Charis, facing Talitha's increasingly dire health crisis, then hearing that Jesus has just landed on your shore. What thoughts, feelings, and hopes do you have?*

Jairus isn't the only one whose hope is kindled by Jesus' arrival. Batya, a woman who's bled for twelve years, comes up behind Jesus with hopes of her own. Having feared that she would live this way forever, Batya tells herself that if she can just touch Jesus' clothes, she will be healed. Unlike Jairus, she doesn't approach him directly. No wonder. Her condition makes her unclean according to biblical law: she is prevented from worshiping at the temple; anyone or anything she touches also becomes unclean, so she is ostracized by her community; she is impoverished, infertile, likely anemic, and probably unmarriageable. And it's been twelve . . . long . . . years.

Batya is hopeless . . . until Jesus lands on her shore.

**REFLECT:** *Put yourself in Batya's sandals, suffering twelve long years of bleeding, then hearing Jesus has landed on your shore. What thoughts, feelings, and hopes do you have?*

Whatever desperation or longing Batya feels, she pushes through the crowds pressed in around Jesus, touches his cloak, and immediately she's healed. Healed before meeting Jesus face-to-face or talking honestly with him, healed without asking or obeying. And if all that mattered was physical healing, this would be a satisfying conclusion to the story. But Jesus wants more for this daughter who has crept up behind him and received healing.

Before she can slip away, Jesus turns around and asks, "Who touched me?"

Batya, who just received a life-transforming miracle, is now surrounded by a curious crowd, impatient men, and a desperate father. In her desire to get well, she has distracted Jesus from dealing with a crisis—the daughter of a very important man is on the brink of death.

Jesus, though, doesn't ask the question once and move on; he keeps looking to see who touched him. His disciples are impatient. *Why ask such a futile question? Look at these crowds!* Yet Jesus, even during a crisis, keeps looking (v. 32). He's not worried or in a hurry. He needs to connect with his daughter, the one hiding and trembling with fear. He keeps looking until he finds her.

When you're a bleeding mess, or what you love most is dying, Jesus lands on your shores. Even when you're living with fear that takes your breath away, it's worth pushing through the crowds to get to him. He's looking for you.

# GOD MEETS US WHERE WE ARE

1. Where in your life do you relate to Batya, suffering a chronic condition? Perhaps you have "spent everything you have" and yet the situation grows worse?

2. Where in your life do you relate to Jairus, who's in crisis mode?

## AN INVITATION: HOLY IMAGINATION

Take a moment to imagine yourself pushing through the crowd to get to the cloak of Jesus. What do you hear? See? Smell? Imagine yourself reaching out to touch his cloak. What are you longing for? What do you notice or feel as you touch his cloak? Write down what you imagine.

# Day 2

## JESUS WELCOMES BATYA
## INTO HONEST CONVERSATION

Unlike Jairus, who felt he could come directly to Jesus with a desperate request, Batya approaches Jesus silently, coming up behind him, and touching only the hem of his garment. Her behavior suggests she doesn't think Jesus would want to interact with her. Why would this amazing rabbi take time to relate to her?

Yet Jesus stops, turns around in the crowd, and asks, "Who touched me?"

> **OBSERVE** *Mark 5:30-33: Describe how Batya responded to Jesus' question. When have you felt such fear your body trembled?*

The text doesn't say how long Jesus looked through the crowd searching for Batya's face. But imagine her terror as she wonders whether she has done something dreadfully wrong. She's felt the power heal her body. But maybe Jesus is mad at her. Maybe he wants his power back. Why else is he so insistent on finding out who touched him?

Batya has a choice about whether she should step forward to tell the truth or hide in the crowd. Amazingly, trembling with fear, Batya steps forward. Like Jairus, she falls at Jesus' feet. And Jesus welcomes her into an honest conversation. What a beautiful line: she "told him the whole truth."

What was this whole truth? It was twelve years spending all she had on doctors and potions, promised cures and dashed dreams; twelve years of being an outcast; twelve long years of being unclean (vv. 25-26). Given her fear, we imagine that Jesus had to coax the story out of her, that the whole truth took some time.

It's astounding that Jesus took so much time with Batya while Jairus stood next to him in the midst of a medical crisis. But Jesus wanted to hear her *whole truth*.

Jesus wants to hear our whole truth too. He wants to hear the ins and outs of what ails us and the long years of worry that nothing will ever get better.

> **REFLECT:** *How does it make you feel to know that Jesus wants to hear the whole truth about your fears and worries?*

Some of us have stories like Batya's, years and years of unresolved pain and sorrow. Others of us have been thrust into a terrifying crisis like Jairus. No matter why we tremble with fear, Jesus has all the time in the world to hear our whole story, and he welcomes us into honest conversation.

## GOD WELCOMES US INTO HONEST CONVERSATION

1. What parts of your "whole truth" have you not shared with Jesus? What has stopped you from sharing?

Jesus is inviting you to tell him your whole truth. Ask him what part he wants to hear. Spend as much time as you'd like sharing your story. You may not have time to tell it all now, but he has as much time as you need.

## Day 3

### JESUS CALLS JAIRUS TO TRUST AND OBEY

Batya trusts and obeys Jesus when she comes forward to admit she touched his cloak. But what about Jairus? What does trust and obedience look like to a parent whose child is on the brink of death? Just when Jesus agrees to go home with Jairus, just as he dares to hope that his daughter may live, they get interrupted—for what must have felt like an eternity, by an unclean woman with a chronic disease. Imagine the panic growing within Jairus, the anger, the frustration, the small spark of hope dimming. Yet we don't see him trying to hurry Jesus along. We don't see him interacting with the woman or reminding Jesus there's a crisis at hand. Somehow, in this most terrifying of moments, Jairus trusts Jesus enough to wait.

> **REFLECT** *on Mark 5:25-34: What would you have done if you were Jairus listening to Jesus and Batya's conversation?*

Fear and waiting go together. Jairus waits for Jesus to finish what he's doing before coming home with him. Charis waits at Talitha's side for Jairus to bring Jesus home. When we're worried, especially for our kids, there's a lot of waiting involved. Waiting for a diagnosis, waiting for a social or academic breakthrough, waiting through the night for a teen to come home. Psalm after Psalm instructs us to wait on the Lord. Trust and obedience often look like having the faith to wait.

In the midst of the dreadful waiting for Batya to finish her story, the news comes that Talitha has died. "Why bother the teacher anymore," the messengers tell Jairus. *There's no reason for Jesus to come back to the house anymore. Let him go on with his business.*

Jesus overhears the conversation and says, "Don't be afraid; just believe." Jesus says, *Let me go with you. Believe that I can be trusted.* For Jairus, obedient faith means letting Jesus come home with him.

> **OBSERVE** *Mark 5:35-43: Describe the scene at Jairus's home and how various folks responded to Jesus.*

At Jairus's house, mourners wail loudly, surrounding Charis who has just watched her child breathe her last. Her husband shows up with the man who didn't come in time to heal her daughter and has the nerve to say to the bereft crowd, "Why all this commotion and wailing? The child is not dead but asleep" (v. 39). How could Charis believe such an outrageous claim? Why didn't she throw him out? Instead, she lets Jesus clear the house of mourners. In an act of incredible trust and obedience, Charis lets Jesus lead her back into the room where hope has just died.

Fear and sorrow can be paralyzing. We freeze and don't know what to do. In those moments, the call to trust and obey is simply to allow Jesus to come home with us and let him take charge from there. Even if it means following him into those rooms where death seems to have won. Transformation—for Talitha, for her parents, and for us—starts by letting Jesus come home with us, moving away from the doorway, and letting him in.

## GOD CALLS US TO TRUST AND OBEY

Where are you waiting, hoping that Jesus will hurry up already?!

### AN INVITATION: INVITING JESUS INTO A ROOM IN YOUR HOUSE

Take one minute and ask the Holy Spirit to show you a "room" where it's difficult to let Jesus enter. Maybe it's your bedroom and sex life. Maybe it's your empty living room with no friends. Maybe it's your car where siblings squabble so fiercely you wonder whether your family will fracture. Or it's your kitchen where there's never enough to sate everybody's hunger. Or the bathroom where you, or your teenager, look in the mirror and see faults where Jesus sees beauty. Is there some place where you have moved from being worried to being hopeless, where it no longer makes sense to let Jesus in?

Next, sit in stillness for a few minutes and invite Jesus into that room. What did you sense? Write down what you experience.

## JESUS TRANSFORMS BATYA AND JAIRUS AND SETS THEM FREE

*Day 4*

Mothers know the daunting obstacles our children face. So we worry. We worry about their physical and emotional safety: we're up at night worried about school shootings, bullying, the effects of social media, and the choices our kids will make around sex, drugs, and drinking while driving. We worry about their futures: will they be able to support themselves, find meaningful work, or keep their faith when they leave the house? In a world that feels so unsafe, how can we not be worried and anxious? After all, sometimes our greatest fears *do* happen.

Yet in Matthew 6, Jesus invites us to reject worry. How is that even possible? Jesus' command "don't worry" can feel frustrating; what do you mean that we're not supposed to worry?

> **OBSERVE** *Matthew 6:25-34: List everything Jesus tells us not to worry about and what we're to do instead of worry.*

What?? We're supposed to deal with our worry by looking at birds and flowers? How's that helpful? It's not helpful if we interpret Jesus as giving us a three-step cognitive therapy plan that looks like this:

**STEP 1:** Think about how God takes care of the birds and flowers.

**STEP 2:** Think about how much more valuable you are than they are.

**STEP 3:** If birds, who are less valuable than you are, have all their needs met, you don't have to worry. God will surely meet your needs.

When we're consumed by worry, this three-step plan doesn't help. Turns out telling ourselves we *shouldn't* feel worried doesn't keep us from worrying.

But what if Jesus isn't asking us to engage in a cognitive exercise? What if Jesus is speaking literally? What if he asks us to pause in the midst of worry and actually look at birds and flowers?

Looking at birds, flowers, and the rest of God's creation compels us to live in the present. We become present to creation, present to ourselves, and present to God. This is important because the present is the only place to meet with God. While God has worked in our past and promises to be with us in our future, God's love can only be experienced in the present because we live in the present.

This discipline of being present is what Jesus encourages when he instructs, "Do not worry about tomorrow, for tomorrow will worry about itself" (v. 34). Most of what we fear is in the future—running out of money, our son not having any friends, our daughter rejecting God. But we are not in our futures, and neither is the grace of God. And when we live in the future through worry, we miss the transforming comfort and provision God offers right now, in the midst of today's troubles and fears.

Modern research has finally caught up with Jesus, showing that anything we do to center ourselves in the present reduces anxiety. We can watch the sun rise or the sun set. We can look at the veins in a maple leaf, our child's eyelashes, or our dog running around the park and experience God in the present. Kathy found throughout her frequent bouts of atheism growing up that contemplating the waves of the ocean or stars in the sky brought her back to God.

Even as we look at the birds or the flowers, Jesus doesn't demand that we banish painful realities and anxious thoughts from our mind. Instead, those realities and fears are transformed in God's presence.

This is what happens for Batya and Jairus. Jesus invites them both to remain in his presence. He invites Batya to come face-to-face with him rather than slipping away quietly. And when others encourage Jairus to leave the teacher alone, Jesus asks to stay together as they walk to Jairus's home. Though Batya and Jairus eventually receive miraculous healing, a different kind of transformation takes place first. Their fear seems to give way to the comfort of simply being in Jesus' presence.

In *This Here Flesh*, Cole Arthur Riley writes:

> God is not criticizing us for being afraid in a world haunted by so many terrors and traumas. I hear Don't be Afraid and hope that it is not a command not to fear but rather the nurturing voice of a God drawing near to our trembling.

# GOD TRANSFORMS US AND SETS US FREE

1. What keeps you from living in the present with Jesus?

2. What would life look like if you were free (or freer) from worry?

— How would you feel? Behave?

— What different decisions would you make?

— What would you stop or start doing?

## AN INVITATION: NATURE BREAK

Take some time today to look at something in the present like birds and flowers. If you can, try to do this for ten minutes, the "dose" suggested by research. Notice the birds' behavior, colors, and sounds. Notice the flowers' colors, shapes, textures, and even movements. Invite Jesus to stand beside you, marveling at his creation. (If the season or the environment doesn't have birds and flowers, notice other nature around you: snow drifts, tree bark, scurrying ants, etc.)

At the end of your time looking, notice how your body feels and what's happening in your mind. Write down what you experienced.

Perhaps take "nature breaks" every day and see what transformation God brings.

# Day 5

## JESUS INVITES BATYA AND JAIRUS TO BE AGENTS OF SHALOM

Jesus invites both Batya and Jairus to become agents of shalom in small but concrete ways. When Jesus invites Batya to share her "whole truth" in front of the crowd rather than privately, he asks her to publicly model what faith in the midst of fear looks like.

> **OBSERVE** *Mark 5:33-34: What did the crowd witness in Batya's interaction with Jesus?*

It's not easy to be a witness. Batya must feel her vulnerability in every way. As a bleeding woman, she's been unclean for twelve years. According to the law in Leviticus 15, anything she touches becomes unclean and any person she touches likewise becomes unclean. She isn't supposed to be in the crowd, let alone touching Jesus, who she's now made unclean. So when, in fear and trembling, Batya dares to tell Jesus her whole truth in front of the crowd, she models and makes space for others to share their own messy stories with Jesus.

God welcomes our private tears and petitions, and it's important to have honest conversations with God outside the spotlight. But when we publicly share our whole truth—including struggles, fears, and sins—as Batya did, we create room for others to share their whole truth. When we dare ask others to pray with us about it all, we bear witness to the kind of God we have in Jesus: one whose grace and love are bigger than our shame and fear. Our public witness makes it easier for others to approach Jesus with their own shame and fear.

When messengers inform Jairus that Talitha has died, Jesus tells him to not be afraid, just believe. So Jairus brings Jesus home to his devastated wife and dead daughter. Despite the mocking of the mourners, Jairus brings Jesus to Talitha. What greater act of shalom is there than bringing Jesus to those we love who are fearful or desperately in need of his touch?

We can't bring the incarnate Jesus to our loved ones like Jairus did. But we can bring the people we love to Jesus through prayer. When our loved ones are suffering or trembling with fear, we can pray with them right then and there. Scripture encourages us that God hears and responds to our prayers. More than that, Psalm 145:18 teaches us that God is "near to all who call on him." We can be confident that when we bring our friends to God in prayer, God is near and God responds.

> **REFLECT:** *Recall a time when someone brought you to God in prayer. What was that like? How did you experience more of God's shalom during or after the prayer?*

So many of our friends, family members, and kids tremble with fear. God can use us to offer them a little more shalom. When we tell them our whole truth like Batya, warts and all, we make a little more room for them to tell their whole truth too. When we bring Jesus to them like Jairus did, we introduce them to the one who can not only heal but raise the dead.

# GOD INVITES US TO BE AGENTS OF SHALOM

1. Where or with whom might God be inviting you to share your vulnerable story?

2. How might sharing your story provide freedom for someone else?

## AN INVITATION: INTERCESSORY PRAYER

Ask the Holy Spirit to bring to mind one person who needs the touch of Jesus. Write down your prayer for them. Text, email, or call and ask if that person would like to meet for prayer.

"Looking at the birds" can be a powerful family sabbath activity. One way to do that is to practice something called *Sit Spot*, developed by Deb Greene-Jacobi. Find one place in God's creation that you can visit regularly and get to know well. It can be a city park or a tree you love. If you have a backyard, that can be a great sit spot. Sit there as a family for three to twenty minutes—depending on the age of your children—and use all of your senses to notice what's around you.

Each person can use a journal to jot things down or draw things they see. They can focus on a flower or anthill or try to take in the whole scene. They can write or draw (or scribble) with as much detail as possible. (Little ones can dictate to parents.) This is not a class, and it's okay if you're not great writers or artists—or if your little ones can't sit still or your teens tell you it's stupid. Be as present as you can, draw, write, and then share and affirm what you each saw. If you don't want to keep a journal, you can ask each person to complete the following sentences:

- I see these five things:
- I hear these four things:
- I feel these three things:
- I smell these two things:
- I taste this one thing:

As you leave, thank God for meeting you in creation.

If you repeat this regularly over the weeks and months, going to your sit spot at different times of day and in all kinds of weather, you will develop a deep sense of presence—with nature and with the God who sustains it all.

# When We're Running From Pain

## GROUP BIBLE STUDY

### CHECK IN ON LAST WEEK

Allow each person to take one to two minutes to share:

— How did your devotionals and family sabbath practice go last week? (No shame or guilt if you didn't get to them.)

— What did you hear (if anything) from God through the studies, the reflection questions, and the invitations?

### INTRODUCTION TO WEEK 3

Have someone read the following aloud:

Motherhood is hard. It involves a ton of pain. The Chinese phrase for enduring suffering—*chi ku*—literally means *eat bitterness*. When life tastes bitter, we often turn to coping mechanisms that we hope will cut the bitterness. We can find ourselves looking for comfort in places that don't ultimately satisfy. Even worse, God's good gifts like food, wine, entertainment, and relationships can lead to addiction when used like a drug to numb the pain and sorrow.

The Samaritan woman in John 4, a woman we will call *Sam*, has had a life of eating bitterness. The good news is that Jesus is waiting for her at the well, ready to offer sweet living water.

### OPENING ACTIVITY

What aspects of mothering make you want to check out or numb yourself? Check all that apply:

☐ the drudgery of diapers, carpools, food prep, etc.

☐ not enough money, time, or energy to meet my children's needs

- ☐ a particularly stressful time of day: getting out of the house in the morning, homework hour, bath time, bedtime, or other times
- ☐ when kids are fighting
- ☐ disagreements between parents about how to handle issues
- ☐ challenges related to children's special needs
- ☐ disobedience, rebelliousness, etc.
- ☐ other: _____

Below is a list of ways moms told us they check out or numb themselves. Select the ones that apply to you.

- ☐ pour a very large glass of wine—it's almost five o'clock, after all
- ☐ head to your room to read a book or binge-watch TV
- ☐ take out your computer and check out what's happening at work
- ☐ hide in the pantry and eat a sleeve of cookies
- ☐ scroll through social media or online shopping offers
- ☐ call a friend to catch up on the latest gossip
- ☐ park the kids in front of a device so they will leave you alone
- ☐ go to the gym to escape having to get the kids ready in the morning
- ☐ other: _____

SHARE with the group what you selected.

VIDEO

WATCH this week's video.

BIBLE STUDY

READ John 4:3-30 aloud.

1. Imagine Sam's initial encounter with Jesus (vv. 4-9):

   — What are some reasons Sam may have gone to the well alone?

   — In addition to water, what else might Sam have needed or wanted?

   — Based on her experience and the tension between Jews and Samaritans, what do you think Sam expected from this strange man?

2. Jesus gives Sam four offers that over time lead to transformation.

   — **To serve him.** "Will you give me a drink?" (v. 7)

     • Why do you think Jesus, the God of the universe, asks Sam to meet his needs?

– **To receive from him.** "If you knew the gift of God and who it is that asks you for a drink, you would have asked him and he would have given you living water." (v. 10)

  • How does she respond to this offer?

  • Since she eventually asks for "this water" (v. 15), what can we assume happened?

– **To bring her painful relationships to him.** "Go, call your husband and come back." (v. 16)

  • How do you think Sam feels when Jesus says this to her?

  • What does it communicate to Sam that Jesus knows all about her past (vv. 17-18) and continues the conversation?

- **To know him as Messiah (or Savior).** "I, the one speaking to you—I am he." (v. 26)

  • This is the first time in the book of John that Jesus reveals to anyone that he is the Messiah! What does this fact tell us about who Jesus came to save?

3. The encounter with Jesus seems to transform Sam in some major ways. When she returns to town (vv. 28-30), how is she different from when she came to the well?

## HOLY SPIRIT CHECK-IN

Take two minutes of silence. Picture yourself going to the well at noon, hoping to avoid the scorn of others. Ask the Holy Spirit to help you identify what you are most thirsty for. What is the water in your life that keeps running out?

Spend another minute to imagine Jesus greeting you at the well. What do you think Jesus wants to offer you? Briefly share what you experience.

## BREATH PRAYER

Take two minutes of silence to practice this breath prayer individually. Then share what, if anything, you experienced while praying. If you feel drawn to this prayer, you can pray it throughout the week.

INHALE: *I am thirsty*

EXHALE: *Give me Living Water*

*Jesus, thank you that you "had" to meet Sam at a well, and that you come to meet us at our wells now. We confess that we use your very good gifts to numb and soothe ourselves in unhealthy ways. We confess that when you offer us Living Water, we choose to drink from wells that leave us thirsty instead. Help us turn to you and receive your Living Water. Help us drink deeply. Amen.*

# Day 1

## JESUS MEETS SAM WHERE SHE IS

John reports that Jesus "had to go through Samaria" (v. 4). Once there, he finds himself alone at a well.

> **OBSERVE** *John 4:4-7: If you were filming a movie of the scene, what details would be important to include?*

There was so much animosity between Jews and Samaritans that rather than walking the straight line between Galilee and Judea, a journey that went through Samaria, Jewish travelers braved the scorching desert to go around Samaria. But not Jesus. Why?

Jesus *has* to go to a well in Samaria because he has a date with Sam.

We're not surprised that Jesus goes to a well to meet Sam. After all, many biblical women met their future husbands at wells: Keturah, Rebekah, Rachel, Zipporah, Asenath, and Tamar. So perhaps Jesus foreshadows that he is coming as the bridegroom—for Sam, her people, and all peoples. More practically, if Jesus wants to meet a Samaritan woman, the town well would be the logical place since women were responsible for obtaining water for their families.

What doesn't make sense is for Jesus to wait for a Samaritan woman at noon. Women drew water for their families in the cool of early morning. When old enough, their daughters drew the water for the family. It was often a social time as friends and neighbors walked together, took turns drawing water, and then carried their heavy loads back home.

But Jesus wants to meet Sam, a woman who comes to the well at noon. He wants to meet Sam, who seems to be avoiding the company and scorn of other women. He wants to meet Sam, who may be longing for respect, a stable marriage, and friendship; who may be mourning the fact that she has no children to get water for her; who may just want to get her water and quickly head home. Jesus wants to meet Sam and waits for her at the right time and the right place.

With Jesus, Sam experiences something new. Jesus never condemns her, never calls her sinful or says she needs forgiveness. Instead, in the midst of the pain and weariness of Sam's life, Jesus initiates a life-transforming relationship with the gentlest of invitations: Will you give me a drink of water?

> **REFLECT:** *Imagine Jesus showing up in your kitchen and asking for a drink of water. What does that feel like?*

Sam's story reminds us that Jesus *has* to come meet us. We, like Sam, may feel alienated and avoid the presence of others. We may be stuck in a pattern that seems inescapable. No matter our vices or habits of avoiding pain, Jesus loves us so much he will always find us, on our soil, at our wells.

## GOD MEETS US WHERE WE ARE

1. What are your wells? Where do you go for relief and nourishment? Where do you flee to when you want to avoid pain?

2. How do you feel knowing that Jesus is waiting at that well to meet with you?

### AN INVITATION: HOLY IMAGINATION

Take a minute to imagine yourself at a well you flee to when you want to numb or escape. Imagine Jesus waiting for you at the well. How does he greet you? Write down what you imagined.

## JESUS WELCOMES SAM
## INTO HONEST CONVERSATION

Sam seems to be an avoider. Even if she did nothing wrong to deserve her marital history, she avoids other women by coming to the well at noon. Yet despite her habit of avoidance, she stays in the conversation with Jesus. In fact, her conversation with Jesus is the longest he has with anyone in the entire book of John! This allows Jesus to address the painful reality at the center of her shame: "Go, call your husband and come back" (v. 16).

> **OBSERVE** *John 4:16-20: Why do you think Jesus wants Sam to call her husband and come back? How did Sam respond to Jesus in verses 17 and 19-20?*

When Sam says that she doesn't have a husband, Sam tells the truth, but not all of it. In response, Jesus makes clear that he already knows her story, including all of her husbands and the man who's not her husband. But Sam isn't ready to share wholly with Jesus. So she changes the subject to historic worship arguments, avoiding the painful truth about why she's at the well alone at noon.

We all know that pain is a part of getting healed: bitter medicine has to be swallowed, broken bones have to be set, cancerous tumors have to be cut out, radiated, or chemically destroyed. Sometimes the cure feels worse than the disease. Kathy's pastor, Christopher, once told a friend, "There's a whole mess of pain you are trying to avoid on your way to what you truly want. But the only way to get to what you want is through the pain. All your avoidance is taking you further and further from what you want." His description, which we've turned into the diagram "The Healing Journey," describes Sam's situation.

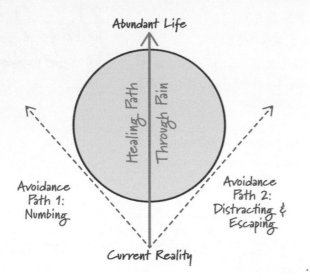

Abundant Life

Healing Path Through Pain

Avoidance Path 1: Numbing

Avoidance Path 2: Distracting & Escaping

Current Reality

THE HEALING JOURNEY

The Healing Journey sketches out the dilemma we all face. We long for an abundant life: to have flourishing children; to do meaningful work; to have healthy bodies, minds, and relationships. Yet our current reality is often far from the abundant life Jesus promises. To get to that abundant life, we must get healed and healing's going to involve some pain. Jesus, our great physician, wants to lead us through that pain on a healing path toward abundance.

That sounds like a lot of work, though, and we're tired. So we attempt to skirt the pain, and instead take avoidance paths through numbing, distracting, or escaping. We soothe ourselves with dessert or park the kids in front of a screen to give ourselves a break. We distract ourselves with online shopping or binge-watching our favorite show. We ignore the hard topics in our marriage by planning an elaborate birthday party, or checking one more thing off our to-do list so we can feel worthy at the end of the day. We seek numbness instead of peace when we open a bottle of wine in the midst of a scary diagnosis. But our avoidance paths don't work. They take us further and further away from abundant life.

> **REFLECT:** *What feelings arise in you as you look at The Healing Journey diagram? Hopefulness? Fear? Anger?*

Jesus finds Sam at the well caught in this dilemma: longing for wholeness and healed relationships but on a path of avoidance that will never get her there. Jesus invites her to get real about her pain as her first step toward healing and abundant life.

Jesus invites us on the same healing journey. When we step off our avoidance paths onto the healing path, he asks us, like Sam, to take that first step by having an honest conversation about our pain and circumstances. As with Sam, he already knows all our longings for abundant life, the suffering we fear to face, and every path of avoidance we keep secret, but he asks us to share anyway. No matter how painful the process, when we share honestly, Jesus can begin to heal us and bring increasing abundant life.

## GOD WELCOMES US INTO
## HONEST CONVERSATION

Put your own words on The Healing Journey diagram. Describe:

— your current reality

— the abundant life you desire

— pain you're afraid of facing on the way to abundant life

— the avoidance paths you take

## AN INVITATION: DISCERNMENT

Sometimes eating cake is a joyful and healthy way to celebrate with friends; other times it's a way of numbing painful emotions. Discerning the difference is part of our healing journey.

Choose a good gift of God from this list: food, relationships, work, exercise, books, entertainment, technology, parties, shopping, and creating beauty.

Next spend a minute asking the Holy Spirit:

— How does this gift nourish me?

— Are there ways I use this gift that hurt me or others?

— What parts of my life might I be avoiding when I use this gift in unhealthy ways?

## JESUS CALLS SAM TO TRUST AND OBEY

*Day 3*

Sam comes to the well seeking H$_2$O. Jesus offers her a different kind of water.

> **OBSERVE** *John 4:10-15: Compare and contrast living water with the water that comes from Jacob's well.*

LIVING WATER AND JACOB'S WATER

| | LIVING WATER | JACOB'S WATER |
|---|---|---|
| What is the water? | | |
| Who gave it? | | |
| How do you get the water? | | |
| How long does the water quench one's thirst? | | |

Jesus' invitation to Sam isn't, "Stop coming here at noon! Face your problems and get your life together!" Instead, he invites her to ask for living water, water that will quench all thirst and give life everlasting. Trusting his offer, Sam asks for this living water. Because Jesus told her that if she asked for living water he would give it to her, surely Jesus gives Sam his living water. What could this amazing water be? John tells us several chapters later.

> **OBSERVE** *John 7:37-39: What did Jesus say about living water? According to John, what did Jesus mean by "living water"? (When John says in verse 39 that believers had not yet received the Spirit, he was referring to Pentecost, when the Spirit would be poured out on all believers.)*

Jesus offers Sam, an outcast Samaritan woman, the Holy Spirit! While the Holy Spirit shows up throughout the Hebrew Bible and in Luke 1, Sam is the first person Jesus offers the gift of the Holy Spirit to in the book of John!

Sam's problems don't magically disappear even after receiving living water, but something has changed. Different faith traditions have wide-ranging views about the Holy Spirit, from virtually ignoring the Spirit to majoring almost solely on the Spirit. Regardless, receiving the indwelling presence of the Holy Spirit brings the power and presence of God into all of Sam's circumstances. With the living water springing up within her, Sam receives the love, encouragement, and power of God to obediently walk the healing path. What a gift!

Jesus offers us this same living water today. Like Sam, all we need to do is ask for it. Empowered by the Holy Spirit, we can face our pain and walk obediently with Jesus down the healing path. He may ask us to regularly tell the truth to a friend, seek counseling and prayer for our emotional wounds, start walking ten minutes a day to de-stress and sleep better, or join a twelve-step group to get sober. Often, he asks us to pause, breathe, and sip some living water.

Whatever the healing path looks like for us, Jesus wants to pour the Holy Spirit into us to encourage, empower, and lead us toward abundant life. Take a pause and ask for living water—it's time for a drink!

## GOD CALLS US TO TRUST AND OBEY

1. How does your faith tradition view the Holy Spirit? What has your experience of the Holy Spirit been?

2. As you think about ways you currently avoid pain, how might asking for a drink of living water—the indwelling presence of the Holy Spirit—require more trust from you?

Ask Jesus for a drink of living water, the power and presence of the Holy Spirit. Then ask the Holy Spirit to show you what the next step on the healing path entails. Write down what you hear.

Keep coming back to ask for more living water, as much as you need as often as you need it.

**Day 4**

## JESUS TRANSFORMS SAM AND SETS HER FREE

Sam's transformation is nothing short of astonishing. Think about it! Sam comes to the well at noon, avoiding other women and the pain their company brings. She leaves so excited she abandons her water jug, runs to the very people she's been avoiding, and boldly shares her testimony.

At every point when Jesus asks Sam to walk the healing path, she says yes: She stays in conversation with him as he presses deeper into her pain. She asks for and receives the Holy Spirit. She accepts his claim that he is the Messiah. She brings her whole town (more than just her "husband"!) out to meet him. Along this healing path, Jesus transforms her, and she is so excited, she can shout it from the rooftops.

Jesus and his disciples spend the next two days in Sychar. For two whole days, Jesus moves into Sam's neighborhood and continues down the healing path with her. John doesn't share all the details of what happened during that time, but knowing Jesus, he just kept on healing and transforming every part of Sam's life.

- As she introduces her community to Jesus, Sam experiences *social healing*. No longer the woman who hides in shame, Sam is now the woman who leads everyone to Jesus, the Messiah.

- As Jesus meets the man Sam lives with and any ex-husbands who are still alive, surely he brings *relational healing*. We imagine Jesus encouraging a time of repentance and forgiveness.

- Finally, as Sam brings Jesus and his slew of Jewish disciples into Sychar, Jesus initiates *ethnic healing* between two groups with deep hatred for one another.

REFLECT: *What areas of your life do you long for Jesus to move into and heal?*

As with Sam, Jesus invites us on a healing journey that transforms us and sets us free. Jesus came so that we could have life abundantly, and he gave his life to make the healing journey possible for anyone who asks. But it's so much easier to run from our pain—numbing ourselves, distracting ourselves, and escaping our reality. We settle for what we have rather than the hope of what God offers. It would have been so much easier for Sam to walk away from this Jewish stranger at the town well than to walk the healing journey. But she trusted and obeyed Jesus and every part of her life was utterly transformed.

## GOD TRANSFORMS US AND SETS US FREE

Recall the abundant life you imagined when sketching out your Healing Journey on day two. To get there, what kind of social, relational, or ethnic healing do you need from Jesus?

### AN INVITATION: THE NEXT STEP

Look again at The Healing Journey diagram and the words you wrote down on day two. Take a minute to ask Jesus what next steps he invites you on in your healing journey. Write down what you hear.

# JESUS INVITES SAM TO BE
# AN AGENT OF SHALOM

*Day 5*

Every part of Jesus' journey to Samaria bears good news, and not just for Sam. That's because when Jesus comes to town, he brings healing, wholeness, and harmony to those he meets. And then he invites those who have experienced his shalom to be bearers of that shalom to others. This was his story with Sam.

Knowing Sam's story of shame and avoidance, Jesus invites her on a healing journey, and chooses her to be the first person in the book of John to:

- be offered the Holy Spirit

- learn his identity as Messiah

- become an evangelist, bringing her whole town to Jesus

Jesus ushers Sam into God's upside-down kingdom, where Samaritan women with messy histories are not only welcome, but become leaders in Jesus' mission of shalom.

By joining Jesus on the healing journey, Sam's pain is not only transformed, the most shameful parts of her story now become her testimony: "He told me everything I ever did" (v. 39). Her freedom and openness must have been compelling because her neighbors, who know her story and have likely scorned her, follow her back to the well to meet Jesus themselves.

> **REFLECT:** *What shameful part of your own story might be the basis of your most powerful testimony?*

Because of Sam's bold witness, Jesus preaches his good news to her entire town, making clear that his kingdom is not only for his people, but for all people, including those who are seen as enemies.

As we noted in day one, wells were places where bridegrooms often met their future brides. But when Abraham's servant went to a well to find a wife for Isaac (Genesis 24), he was looking for a wife from *within* their family. In John 4, Jesus sits beside another well, waiting for another "bride," this time from outside the family. Imagine that. Jesus chose Sam, who likely had no biological children and experienced the grief and isolation of infertility, to be the spiritual mother who birthed the first children of the Gentile church!

This must have come as quite a surprise to his disciples, who needed their own transformation.

> **OBSERVE** *John 4:27-41: How did the disciples react to Sam? How do you think they felt when Jesus announced they were staying two more days in Sychar?*

The disciples are surprised, and not in a good way, when they see Jesus talking with Sam, but they don't ask Jesus their questions. Sam leaves, and Jesus begins answering the disciples' unasked questions by explaining the kind of harvest God wants. As Jesus says to his disciples, "I tell you, *open your eyes* and look at the fields! They are ripe for harvest" (v. 35, emphasis added). What shock and maybe even horror arises as the disciples see the harvest—Sam's neighbors, their enemies—walking toward them!

Then Jesus decides to stay two whole extra days. During those two days in Sychar, Sam, her neighbors, and Jesus' disciples eat together, learn from Jesus together, and pray together. Jesus promised Sam that in his kingdom, all people will worship together. In Samaria, his people took a first step toward fulfilling that promise.

Sam brought Jesus to her neighbors. Her neighbors welcomed Jesus to their town. And the disciples' sojourn in Samaria was a first step toward them preaching the gospel to every nation. Sam and the disciples became agents of the kingdom of God, agents of shalom.

> **REFLECT:** *Think of places that people in your church or community won't go because "those people" are there. How would you feel if Jesus invited you to spend two days in their neighborhood?*

When motherhood stretches our capacities, our energy, and our patience, we often yield to the cold comfort of our favorite escapes, drinking from wells that leave us parched. In those moments, Jesus invites us to take a drink of his living water, to walk with him, crossing all sorts of boundaries, along the healing path toward abundant life and shalom.

# GOD INVITES US TO BE
# AGENTS OF SHALOM

What boundary lines is Jesus crossing in your world? How might you follow him there?

## AN INVITATION: SHARING YOUR STORY

Take a minute to ask the Holy Spirit who you can share your story with. Write their name here and ask the Holy Spirit what a next step might be—a prayer, a short text, a card, or a word the next time you see them.

Introduce your family to a wonderful practice of being present to God: savoring. You need not talk with your children about avoiding pain and turning to wells that run dry. Instead, you can help them learn to savor God's gifts as they were intended to be enjoyed and not as a means of avoidance. With practice, even young children can learn to savor.

Explain that for this sabbath, you are going to savor one of God's great gifts—delicious food.

1. Choose something the whole family likes—like chocolate chip cookies.

2. Invite everyone to put away all distractions. Pray, "God, thank you for your presence with us. And thank you for the gift of cookies."

3. Enjoy the cookies with all your senses except taste. Let everyone share what they see, smell, feel, and even hear (what does it sound like when you drop it on a plate, or cut it with a knife?).

4. Next, ask everyone to take one bite, letting it linger for a bit in their mouths.

5. Most kids will rebel at this point if they must wait much longer, so dig in!

6. Thank God again for being present as you enjoyed such a yummy gift.

# When We're Caught in a Comparison Trap

## GROUP BIBLE STUDY

### CHECK IN ON LAST WEEK

Allow each person to take one to two minutes to share:

- How did your devotionals and family sabbath practice go last week? (No shame or guilt if you didn't get to them.)

- What did you hear (if anything) from God through the studies, the reflection questions, and the invitations?

### INTRODUCTION TO WEEK 4

Have someone read the following aloud:

As mothers, we can feel like we're stuck in an inescapable trap of comparing ourselves to others. And when we compare ourselves to other moms, we end up in a no-win situation. If we think we're better, we judge them; if we think we're worse, we envy them. And when we compare ourselves to an internal standard of what we should be, we judge ourselves mercilessly. In all ways, comparison steals our joy.

The joy-stealing power of comparison is not new. The biblical sisters Leah and Rachel took comparison to a whole new level. These two sisters spent their entire lives judging and envying one another. Tragically, their sister wars led to sexual exploitation, power games, and sibling hatred, consequences that were felt for generations to come.

### OPENING ACTIVITY

Moms in our survey had a lot to say about comparison, judgment, and envy. As you read through the following responses, check any that resonate with you, even if the details don't quite match:

- ☐ There's so much guilt—all the mommy guilt.
- ☐ I feel judged for having a different parenting approach.

☐ There is so much mom competition.

☐ I envy the mothers who have it all: husbands, money, hired help.

☐ I'm constantly judging myself.

☐ Strangers think my kids are not mine because they have a different skin color, and the judgmental things they say hurt so much.

☐ I feel disrespected because I am divorced.

☐ My child is struggling with an issue that I *never* envisioned, and that most other Christians would judge me about.

☐ I feel like I'm the only one who is incompetent.

☐ I have to fight against the lie that I'm a bad mom and I was never meant to be a mom because I couldn't conceive naturally.

☐ Social media makes me feel worse about my parenting and my children.

☐ other: _____

SHARE with the group one or two responses you checked.

VIDEO

WATCH this week's video.

BIBLE STUDY

1. READ Genesis 29:31–30:24 aloud. As you read, fill in the following chart of moms, children, and the meaning of their names. (Hint: Look in the footnotes of the biblical text to get the definitions of the names.)

2. What words would you use to describe the dynamic between the two sisters as they vie for Jacob's love and the ability to bear children?

3. God appears in verses 29:31, 30:17, and 30:22.

   − What does God do?

| MOM | CHILDREN | MEANING OF CHILDREN'S NAMES |
|---|---|---|
| Leah | Reuben | |
| | Simeon | |
| | Levi | |
| | Judah | |
| | Issachar | |
| | Zebulun | |
| | Dinah | |
| Bilhah | Dan | |
| | Naphtali | |
| Zilpah | Gad | |
| | Asher | |
| Rachel | Joseph | |
| | Ben-Oni/ Benjamin | Son of my trouble/son of my right hand (From Genesis 35:18, which we didn't read.) |

— What do we learn about God's character from this?

4. How does the competition between Rachel and Leah affect Bilhah, Zilpah, and the children they bear?

5. There's no evidence of reconciliation between the sisters. What do you wish they would have done to create a healthier family?

6. How has comparing yourself to others affected your relationships in your family of origin? With your children? Other moms?

## HOLY SPIRIT CHECK-IN

Take two minutes to ask what the Spirit wants to show you about the ways comparison, judgment, and envy show up in your relationships. Briefly share what you experienced.

Take two minutes of silence to practice this breath prayer individually. Then share what, if anything, you experienced while praying. If you feel drawn to this prayer, you can pray it throughout the week.

> INHALE: *I struggle with my sister\**

> EXHALE: *Lord bless her*

*\*Could be your actual sister, sister on social media, or woman in the park.*

## LEADER BENEDICTION

*God, we confess that we are caught in a no-win trap of comparison that steals our joy. We judge other moms, and when we're not judging them, we envy them. We judge ourselves, even as we long to see ourselves and others as you see us, fearfully and wonderfully made. Help us to turn from being critics to becoming agents of shalom. Help us to bless and encourage other moms, as you bless and encourage us. Amen.*

## GOD MEETS LEAH AND RACHEL WHERE THEY ARE

*Day 1*

Leah and Rachel aren't great role models for mom-to-mom relationships. They have big feelings about their circumstances and toward one another that never seem to resolve. Yet God meets each of them in the midst of their misery and sibling rivalry.

Leah is unloved and bears the pain of that truth. We can only imagine how Leah felt her first married morning when Jacob took one look at her and stormed off to her father. His rejection had to have been soul-crushing. And then a week later, Jacob marries her sister Rachel, the one he loves and has worked seven years for, and Leah has to live with that painful contrast for years to come.

Yet in the midst of Leah's pain and shame, God sees, enables, and listens to her. Genesis 29:31 says that God *saw* that Leah was unloved. The Hebrew word *s'nuah*, unloved, is usually translated as "hated." Jacob may hate Leah, but God loves her and shows up right where she is. God *sees* that she's hated, so God *enables* Leah to receive the greatest gift a woman could receive in that time, a son.

Many children later, Leah's hopes remain unmet—she's still unloved by Jacob and still comparing herself to Rachel.

Rachel seems to control who sleeps with Jacob, thereby preventing Leah from bearing more children. When Leah's son Reuben finds mandrakes, and Rachel asks for some, Leah spits out, "Wasn't it enough that you took away my husband? Will you take my son's mandrakes too?" (v. 15). Rachel trades one night with Jacob for the mandrakes. How humiliating for Leah to have to demand from Jacob, "You must sleep with me. . . . I have hired you with my son's mandrakes" (v. 16).

Despite how unloved Leah still feels, God has not abandoned her. Even though we never see Leah praying or asking God for anything, God *listens* to Leah and gives her another son in Genesis 30:17. Perhaps God hears her pain. El Roi, the God who saw and heard Hagar, now sees, enables, and listens to Leah.

God comes not only to Leah, who feels *unloved*, God also comes to Rachel, who feels *unworthy* because she's infertile. She's deeply loved by Jacob, but her husband's adoration doesn't cover the pain of infertility. In their culture, a woman's worth was primarily based on her ability to bear children. She sees Leah bearing sons and feels so envious she threatens Jacob, "Give me children, or I'll die!" (Genesis 30:1). In the midst of her jealousy and desperation, God *remembers* Rachel, *listens* to her, and *enables* her to conceive her own son.

> **OBSERVE** *Genesis 30:22-24: What two things does Rachel say after giving birth to her son? How does her first comment give us a window into the deep shame she's felt all along?*

God meets both sisters in the midst of their misery. Despite their pettiness and competition, even though we never see them seek God or even ask for God's assistance, God shows up and is merciful to them. God *sees*, *enables*, *listens*, and *remembers*.

What good news that God meets these mothers where they are, in all their brokenness. God has compassion on Leah and Rachel, and God has compassion on us as well. Even when we feel unloved or unworthy. Even when we can't stop comparing ourselves to others. When we're consumed with envy or caught in a storm of judgment, our God sees, enables, listens, and remembers.

## GOD MEETS US WHERE WE ARE

1. Who do you relate to more, Leah or Rachel?

2. Where have you felt unloved? Unworthy?

**AN INVITATION: HOLY SPIRIT PAUSE**

God sees your situation and hears your misery. God remembers your longings. Ask the Holy Spirit to show you what God sees, hears, and remembers. Write down what you hear.

*Day 2*

## LEAH AND RACHEL MISS THE OPPORTUNITY TO HAVE AN HONEST CONVERSATION WITH GOD

Have you had a friend who listens deeply? A friend who waits patiently while you get the whole story out, who can follow you along the twists and turns as you figure out what you need to say, and who asks just the right questions to let you know they're listening, no matter how long it takes? If so, then you know what a gift it is that God listens to Rachel and Leah. But God isn't only listening; God longs for them to engage.

There is no greater invitation to talk honestly than the presence of someone who truly wants to listen to what you have to say.

**REFLECT:** *Think of a friend or family member who is a really good listener and all of the ways they make it safe to open up to them. How does that compare with your experience of God as listener?*

Leah and Rachel could both benefit from a good listener and confidant. They need a friend to listen to them as they weep over their heartbreak. They need someone to vent with about the pain and shame their culture creates by equating their worth to what they look like or how fertile they are. They need a trusted confidant who will listen to their confessions as they're caught in the downward spiral of comparison and envy.

**OBSERVE** *Genesis 29:31–30:24: List instances of Rachel or Leah talking to God. List instances of them talking about God.*

We don't know what Leah's and Rachel's relationship with God was like, if they prayed, or if they experienced God's presence. We never see them taking up God's offer for honest conversation. Instead, they often use God's name as a weapon in their war of misery, spewing out hateful feelings in their messages: *I won! You lose! Look at how much God loves me! God is on my side.*

Too often we think God is good when we get what we want, and evil, silent, or indifferent when we don't. But God is never evil, silent, or indifferent. God invites us to honestly share about everything in our lives, and when we do, we experience God's loving presence and come to know God's character. Even when God says no or not yet.

What might have changed if Leah and Rachel poured out their true feelings to God? What if they had prayed:

- Why God, why? Why is my sister beautiful while I have weak eyes?
- Lord, it hurts so much to be unloved.
- I feel so jealous of my sister and her children that I want to scratch her eyes out.
- God, my sister's making me miserable.
- Lord, it's humiliating to have to beg my husband to make love to me.

What if instead of talking *about* God—using God's name as proof that they are winning—Leah and Rachel talked *to* God, deepening their relationship with their Father in heaven? What if they pushed through any fears they may have had that God was indifferent to or even relished their pain? What if either of them responded to their pain by talking honestly with God directly? How might that have broken them free from the comparison trap?

Instead, they pour out their feelings in the names they give their sons. The competition between them comes out most obviously when Rachel names Bilhah's son *Naphtali*, saying, "I have had a great struggle with my sister, and I have won" (30:8). Even when she bears her own son, he's not enough. She names him *Joseph*, meaning "may he add another." They act as if their children, Zilpah, and Bilhah are mere pawns in their battle for love and worth. Their constant comparison diminishes the joy they may experience and creates extreme family dysfunction.

Like Leah and Rachel, when we feel insecure about our belovedness or worth, it's easy to fall into comparison, judgment, and envy. This temptation grows when we become mothers and add children into the equation, using our children as part of our own mommy wars. Whose kid slept through the night first? Whose kid scored the last-minute goal or got into the best college? Whose kid is more popular, leads their youth group, or is more likely to befriend the new kid? There is almost nothing we can't use as a means of comparison—feeling judgmental and superior when we "win," and envious and crappy when we "lose." And because these emotions often feel shameful, we keep them secret. But telling God the truth about how we feel opens these hidden places to the fresh breath of the Holy Spirit. God is listening and invites us to honestly share the whole ugly truth about our deepest insecurities and the ways we judge and envy.

When you feel unloved or unworthy, share it with God.

## GOD WELCOMES US INTO HONEST CONVERSATION

1. Do you have an easier time talking *to* God or *about* God? How does that change when you are feeling unloved or unworthy?

2. In what ways do you judge yourself or other moms? In what ways do you envy other moms?

*Day 3*

## GOD CALLS LEAH AND RACHEL TO TRUST AND OBEY

Perhaps the deepest longing of the human heart is to be seen, known, and chosen. Leah and Rachel respond to these unmet longings through comparison, envy, and sister wars.

God offers us a different way.

Rather than comparing ourselves with other moms and feeling either superior or inferior, God invites us to trust that we are each fully loved and deeply worthy. Psalm 139 gives us a picture of God's abundant love for us and how, because God knit every cell in our bodies together, we can revel in our worth.

**OBSERVE** *Psalm 139:1-18:*

*In verses 1-6, notice all the different ways that God knows you.*

In verses 7-12, list all the ways God goes with you.

In verses 13-18, list all the ways you are fearfully and wonderfully made.

We are God's beloved daughters, carefully formed and created by our Father God. Each of us is unique and precious. God lovingly wove us together in the depths of our mothers' wombs. When our mothers couldn't yet see our features or know our particularities, God already did. We are not a mistake.

We can trust in God's love and God's character. Verse 17 can be translated "How amazing are your thoughts concerning me, God. How vast the sum of them!" Can you imagine God having infinite precious thoughts about you? God knows every thought in our minds, every movement of our bodies, and every word on our lips before we speak them. God sees it all and loves us. God wants to wash away our insecurities with an ocean of love that is vast, unending, and all-encompassing. God does not compare you to the mom next door.

> **REFLECT:** *How do you think things would have been different between Rachel and Leah if they had trusted that they were fearfully and wonderfully made?*

What if Leah and Rachel hadn't fallen prey to comparison? What if they believed that God had knit them together in their mother's womb, that they were each fearfully and wonderfully made? What if, at the birth of their children, they believed the same thing for each child? Could they have responded in gratitude rather than comparison?

As we trust that God has made each of us unique and beautiful, the obedient response according to Psalm 139 is praise (v. 14). We praise God because we are fearfully and wonderfully made, a wonderful work of God. This was true for Leah, for Rachel, and it's true for each one of us, and each one of our children. We are seen, known, loved, and chosen. Praise God!

# GOD CALLS US TO TRUST AND OBEY

1. What would change if you trusted that you were fearfully and wonderfully made? That your children were?

2. What would change if you trusted that the moms you judge or envy were also fearfully and wonderfully made?

3. How could praise, as an obedient response to God's love for you, help you when you are in a spiral of envy and self-judgment?

## *Day 4*

## THE HOLY SPIRIT TRANSFORMS AND SETS MARY AND ELIZABETH FREE

Sadly, there's little transformation or freedom in Leah and Rachel's stories. Their well-being depends on how Jacob feels about them or how fertile they are. Their relationship to God is reduced to whether they get what they want. Their envy, judgment, and competition never seem to resolve. In contrast, let's look at another pair of mothers—Elizabeth and Mary, two cousins who both receive miraculous pregnancies from God.

> **OBSERVE** *Luke 1:5-80: Rather than being filled with envy or judgment, how do Elizabeth and Mary interact with one another in verses 39-56?*

Elizabeth and Mary could have followed the path of Leah and Rachel. Elizabeth could have pouted that Mary's son would be greater than hers or wagged her finger at her unwed cousin. Mary could have gloated that she carried the Messiah or envied that Elizabeth's miraculous pregnancy brought glory instead of shame. Instead of comparison, envy, or judgment, Mary and Elizabeth respond to God's initiative with support of one another and praise to God.

How is that possible? We read that Elizabeth is righteous and faithful (v. 6), but even the faithful can fall into the trap of comparison. Perhaps the truth that they are fearfully and wonderfully made sank deep within their psyches as they regularly prayed Psalm 139 over their lifetimes; God certainly uses Scripture to transform our character. What we see in Luke, though, is the kind of miraculous freedom that comes from being filled with the Holy Spirit.

> **OBSERVE:** *Find every mention of the Holy Spirit (or Spirit) in Luke 1 and fill in the chart.*

THE FILLING OF THE HOLY SPIRIT IN LUKE 1

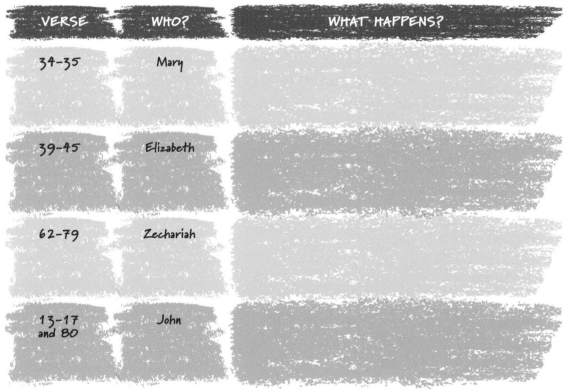

| VERSE | WHO? | WHAT HAPPENS? |
|---|---|---|
| 34–35 | Mary | |
| 39–45 | Elizabeth | |
| 62–79 | Zechariah | |
| 13–17 and 80 | John | |

The filling of the Holy Spirit leads to so much good news: John brings reconciliation between parents and children. Mary gives birth to the Son of God. Elizabeth blesses Mary, her cousin and fellow mom. Mary and Zechariah praise and prophesy about God's goodness.

As we saw with Sam in last week's study, when the Holy Spirit fills us, we get transformed. Scripture confirms this repeatedly. Jesus promised that the Holy Spirit would live within us, teach us, and remind us of God's goodness (John 14). At Pentecost, the filling of the Holy Spirit gave Jesus' followers the courage to boldly praise God and speak God's wonders—in every language!—in the place that only weeks earlier, Jesus had been crucified. Faith and boldness replace fear, and joy replaces sorrow (Acts 2). The apostle Paul writes to the Galatian church that the fruit of the Holy Spirit is love, joy, peace, patience, kindness, goodness, faithfulness, gentleness, and self-control (Galatians 5:22-23). As we're filled with the Spirit, we are transformed in every way.

Without the filling of the Holy Spirit, Mary and Elizabeth might have been, like Leah and Rachel, caught in the trap of comparison. But with the Holy Spirit, they are free to enjoy God, their pregnancies, and their friendship. That same freedom is available to us when we ask the Spirit to fill us and grow the fruit of the Spirit within us.

## GOD TRANSFORMS US AND SETS US FREE

The Holy Spirit wants to transform you and free you from the comparison trap. What relationship or situation most needs the power of the Holy Spirit right now?

Ask the Holy Spirit to fill you and give you the power to bless and praise rather than compare, judge, or envy. Write down what you experienced.

## GOD INVITES MARY AND ELIZABETH TO BE AGENTS OF SHALOM

Leah and Rachel. Elizabeth and Mary. The depth of their emotions is palpable. Their longings—to be seen and known by God and community, to be loved and cherished by God and husband, to bear and nurse and nurture babies—feel achingly familiar. How each pair responds to their longings determines the fate of generations to come.

Leah and Rachel never seem to trust God in the midst of their suffering, even coveting false idols for security (Genesis 31). Their comparisons rob them of the joys of children and sisterhood. Eventually, because their pain is untransformed, all the injustices committed against them lead to even more horrible injustices. They use the little power they have to sexually exploit their servants Bilhah and Zilpah. Unlike Hagar, who got to keep her son, Bilhah and Zilpah's sons aren't even counted as their own.

REFLECT: *There are four mothers described in Genesis 29 and 30, yet we only get to hear the experiences of two of them in detail. Write down what you imagine it felt like to be Bilhah and Zilpah in this story.*

The envy and judgment from Rachel's and Leah's childhood intensifies in marriage and parenting, then overflows to the next generation. Leah, Bilhah, and Zilpah's sons hate Rachel's son Joseph because their father loves him the most (Genesis 37:4). Their hatred culminates in their plot to kill him (Genesis 37:19-20).

In contrast, for Elizabeth and Mary, blessing and love flow down in the same way that comparison and hatred did for Leah and Rachel. In Luke 1:41-45, upon hearing Mary's greeting, Elizabeth is filled with the Holy Spirit, so filled that she's compelled to shout blessings over Mary: "Blessed are you among women, and blessed is the child you will bear!"

Think of all the goodness that flows out of Elizabeth's initial blessing of Mary: Mary praises God and prophesies about Jesus and his kingdom. Elizabeth's blessing of Mary goes beyond mere words; she takes in Mary and shelters her for three months. As Mary, pregnant before wedlock, faces the threat of stoning, being sheltered by a priest's family provides both emotional and physical safety. Eventually, Elizabeth's son baptizes Mary's son, and both sons usher in a kingdom of shalom. Shalom flows from God to these two mothers and on down through eternity.

REFLECT: *When have you experienced an outpouring of blessing like Elizabeth and Mary did? What was that like?*

Isn't it encouraging that as the Holy Spirit fills us, like Elizabeth, we're empowered to bless other moms? God's blessing is so abundant that when we don't dam it up with judgment and envy, it transforms and frees those around us.

Day to day, sometimes moment to moment, we can find ourselves identifying with one pair of mothers or the other. Trapped in comparison like Rachel and Leah, we scroll through social media, wondering why our families don't look like the families we so admire. Envy, competition, and judgment rise in our craw. Our gossip creates toxic environments. Other moms feel unsafe around us.

In our best moments, we experience the freedom and joy of Mary and Elizabeth. Friendships based on mutual blessing allow us to see ourselves, each other, and God more clearly. We praise God for one another. We bless other mothers, becoming a cheering section like the crowds that line the road during a marathon: "You can do it! Looking good! Just a little farther! Keep it up!" Like Elizabeth, we can bless and shelter the vulnerable. When we follow the path of Mary and Elizabeth, together, we moms become agents of shalom, raising a new generation of shalom-bearers. May God's shalom flow from our families into eternity.

## GOD INVITES US TO BE AGENTS OF SHALOM

1. Where does your family history include generational comparison and competition? Generational blessing and shelter? What are the consequences of those legacies?

2. In what relationships would you love to see a flow of blessing rather than comparison, envy, and judgment? What first step could you take to begin the flow of blessing?

## AN INVITATION: SAYING NO TO GOSSIP

Too often women bond by sharing judgments about others, criticizing and tearing other mothers down in the form of gossip. Ask God to help you speak of other moms in ways you wouldn't be ashamed for them to overhear. Write your prayer below.

This week, play a game our friend Becca calls "Spot the Lie." Our children ingest a constant drip of lies from the culture around them, many of them based on beliefs about what will make us feel loved, worthy, or happy. Because those erroneous beliefs can't actually deliver love, worth, or happiness, they leave us wanting more, feeling inadequate, and experiencing envy. Those beliefs make it difficult to experience true joy, which happens when we find love, worth, and happiness through our identities in Jesus. Learning to spot the lies that steal our true joy can become an important family discipline.

If your family sabbath includes media use, change into your comfy clothes, pop some popcorn, and get cozy. You can watch a movie, a TV program, or even online videos, and look for a lie while you are watching. You might see it in a commercial that promises nonstop joy if you buy a certain toy. Or in a program that conveys that romance is the essence of love. The more subtle lies—that you are what you accomplish, or lies about gender and race and beauty—can be harder to spot. Over time, though, your children will be shouting "That's a lie!" even when you are not officially playing the game.

Because all good art also conveys truth, it will be important to play "Spot the Gospel" on another day. We might see a movie where a character is valued and loved simply for being someone's beloved. We might hear a hit song where sacrifice is valued over worldly success. Spotting beauty and truth can be harder than spotting lies. Training our eyes to see the good work of God all around us is a discipline all its own. Again, after doing this for even a short time, your family just might be heard shouting "That's the gospel!" every time you sit down to enjoy a great movie.

*Family Sabbath*

# When We're Angry

## GROUP BIBLE STUDY

### CHECK IN ON LAST WEEK

Allow each person to take one to two minutes to share:

— How did your devotionals and family sabbath practice go last week? (No shame or guilt if you didn't get to them.)

— What did you hear (if anything) from God through the studies, the reflection questions, and the invitations?

### INTRODUCTION TO WEEK 5

Have someone read the following aloud:

For those of us who wrestle with anger, the good news is that God also gets angry. Anger is part of how we reflect God's image and, like fire, a gift from God when held in the proper context. God gave us anger so that when danger comes, we become mama bears who can fend off attackers, defend the vulnerable, and fight injustice. Unfortunately, the good fire God gives to light the way can also burn out of control. No matter how we typically express our anger, God invites us to listen to it and use it in ways that give life to us and our communities. In this study, we examine anger through the story of Herodias, a mother whose angry grudge leads to murder.

### OPENING ACTIVITY

If your anger were a fire, how would you describe it?

- ☐ held in its proper context, providing light and energy where needed
- ☐ burning like a wildfire, destroying everything in its path
- ☐ swallowed and burning slowly within
- ☐ bottled up, like a Molotov cocktail that might explode if dropped
- ☐ nursed along and banked, waiting for the right moment to ignite

VIDEO

WATCH this week's video.

BIBLE STUDY

READ Mark 6:17-29 aloud.

1. How does Herodias respond to John's message?

2. With Herodias's family history in mind, why do you think John's message triggers her the way it does?

3. How do you think God saw Herodias? What do you think God was offering her through John's message of judgment and repentance?

4. Herodias doesn't seem to seek transformation. Instead, she clings to her pain.

   — How does the Bible describe that in verse 19?

— What does it take to "nurse a grudge"? What was the result of her grudge?

5. What resentments and grudges have you received from your parents? Which of these are you passing on to your kids?

## HOLY SPIRIT CHECK-IN

Take one minute with the Holy Spirit to get curious about your anger. Ask if there is anything about your anger the Spirit wants you to notice and explore. Briefly share what you experienced.

## BREATH PRAYER

Take two minutes of silence to practice this breath prayer individually. Then share what, if anything, you experienced while praying. If you feel drawn to this prayer, you can pray it throughout the week.

INHALE: *In my anger*

EXHALE: *Help me not sin*

## LEADER BENEDICTION

*God, we confess that in our anger we sin. Sometimes we rage, hurting others and breaking relationships. Sometimes we ignore our holy anger and don't act on behalf of ourselves and others. And other times, we swallow our anger, hold a grudge, and seethe with bitterness. Forgive us God. Teach us to use anger righteously, for the sake of your glory and the shalom of the world. Amen.*

# Day 1

## GOD SENDS A PROPHET TO HERODIAS

Growing up in a family where power and position trumped familial love and loyalty, Herodias experienced loads of trauma in her childhood. When she was eight, her grandfather, Herod the Great, murdered her father. Soon after, she was married off to her uncle Philip. Herodias grew up with little control over her life, family, or circumstances. Given her history, perhaps she felt like she deserved her chance for happiness when she divorced her uncle and married his brother with whom she'd fallen in love.

Into this tangle of trauma, sin, anger, and passion, God shows up. God sends a prophet to show Herod Antipas and Herodias a different way.

> **OBSERVE** *Mark 6:17-20: What message does God send Herodias and Herod through John?*

Even though John has spent years inviting people to repent and be forgiven, Herodias doesn't hear John's critique that way. She hears it as a threat and nurses a grudge, a grudge that perpetuates her family's cycle of exploitation and murder.

Perhaps John's message provokes Herodias's anger because it threatens all three of her basic needs: love, security, and agency. (By agency, we mean a sense that we can act in ways that will lead to meaningful change, a sense that we are not completely controlled by our circumstances.) Maybe her marriage gives her what she always longed for but never had: true love, security in a world where fathers murder sons, and agency in a life controlled by powerful men. If so, then no wonder she feels murderous rage. How dare John threaten her newfound happiness and rile up the people about her relationship? Does he know what she's been through? Why should she have to repent? Whatever good plans God might have for her future can't be trusted compared to what she has now.

> **REFLECT:** *What emotions come up for you when God sends someone to ask you to repent of your sin?*

Even when we haven't been confronted by a prophet with our sin, we can still find ourselves insanely angry. Why? Often because, like Herodias, when our primal needs for love, security, or agency have been threatened, we react with a fight, flight, or freeze response. Anger is the fight response, and while it is an important emotion that can spur us to act justly on behalf of ourselves and others, it can also lead us astray.

Think here of Tara, terrified that her dyslexic son will always struggle to read, triggered by her need for security, glaring at him in unspoken rage and spitting out, "Just copy down what it says! It's not that hard!" Or picture Kathy—driving while her four-year-old tantrums and screams, "I hate you! You're the most terrible mom! You're poop and I want to flush you down the toilet!"—so triggered by her need for control that she screeches to a halt, pulls this child out of the minivan, and threatens to leave her on the sidewalk.

In those moments when our needs are not met and anger leads us astray, we can see our feelings as a cue from God, a gift God gives us to pay attention to something serious in our lives, a place God longs to meet us. If we receive our anger as God's invitation to walk together through whatever is making us so mad, we can listen to our anger with appreciation and curiosity. It may be the stirring of the Holy Spirit, meeting us where we are.

## GOD MEETS US WHERE WE ARE

1. What makes you feel angry or, like Kathy and Tara, insanely angry?

2. For Herodias, power and position trumped love in her family of origin. Were there things that trumped love in your family of origin? Do those very things sometimes ignite anger in you today?

### AN INVITATION: TIME OUT

Toddlers aren't the only ones who can benefit from a time out. Take a time out to be alone with God when your anger is getting the best of you. Feel free to vent, cry out, or even have a temper tantrum with God. Imagine yourself pounding your fists on Jesus' chest. Taking just a few minutes to step away and be with God can re-center you, reminding you that you are beloved even when your behavior isn't lovely.

# GOD WELCOMES HONEST CONVERSATION

We moms will confess many sins to one another before we confess that we have completely lost it on our children. It's off-limits, which puts us in a bind: we need forgiveness and encouragement when we react sinfully in our anger, but our inability to stop causes us to hide in our shame.

A passage in James can help us come out of hiding with God about our anger by helping us understand its origins. James begins chapter four by asking what causes fights and quarrels. If your households are like ours, this question certainly feels relevant.

> **OBSERVE** *James 4:1-3: What does James say about quarrels and fighting?*

So many desires battle within us, desires for flourishing marriages, healthy kids, good work, and life-giving friendships. Beneath these desires lie our God-given primal needs for love, security, and agency. God knows these needs and God wants to meet them. Yet when we worship love, security, or agency more than we worship God, our desire for these good gifts becomes disordered; we want the gift more than we want the gift giver. The biblical word for a gift we want more than God is *idol*. That's what happened with Herodias, Sarah, Leah, and Rachel—their desires for good things became disordered and they made idols out of marital love and children. When their idols were threatened, they acted out in horrible ways.

Talking honestly with God about our disordered desires and idols can be scary. Some of us have been chasing those idols for a long time. We've sacrificed mightily to get them when and how we want them. And we fear that if we start talking honestly to God about them, God will take them away.

Maybe this is why we never see Herodias, Sarah, Leah, or Rachel talking to God: they idolized human relationships more than God and didn't want God interfering with their business. What might have happened if Herodias had taken John's warning seriously and, like her husband, gone to the prison to ask John more about his message and to tell him her side? What if she had cried out to God that John's message felt unjust, admitted how much she wanted her new relationship, or confided the deep shame John's words provoked? How might God have responded to her?

Talking honestly with God opens us up to the power of the Holy Spirit, our helper. James reminds us at the end of verse 2 to ask God directly for help when the battles within lead to anger. Just as we (generally) don't abandon our toddlers when they're having a tantrum, God is right there when we are angry and even when we are out of control. Talk honestly with God, even if it means throwing a tantrum. God can handle it.

## GOD WELCOMES US INTO
## HONEST CONVERSATION

Picture the quarrels in your house as the tip of the iceberg. The battling desires that cause the quarrels lie beneath the surface.

*Quarrels*

*Battling Desires*

In your home, what part of the iceberg can everyone see? What desires lie beneath the surface?

**AN INVITATION: IDENTIFYING YOUR DESIRES**

Take a moment to ask the Holy Spirit to help you recognize the desires of your heart: for yourself, your kids, your relationships, your work, your community. Write down what you hear. Without judging your list, share it with God.

**Day 3**

## GOD CALLS HERODIAS
## TO TRUST AND OBEY

Herodias could have responded to John's message with trust and obedience. Instead, she attempts to meet her God-given needs for love, security, and agency on her own. When Herodias was caught in the spiral of shame, anger, and bitterness, what would it have taken for her to release her needs to God, trusting that God would fulfill them? In Matthew 6, Jesus addresses this question.

> **OBSERVE** *Matthew 6:31-33: What does Jesus say to encourage his listeners to release their needs to God?*

While Jesus directly addresses our need for security in this passage, his words apply to our needs for love and agency as well. We don't have to run after any of these things because our heavenly Father already knows we need them. Jesus instead asks us to seek first his kingdom and righteousness and trust that all our needs will be supplied. But how do we do this?

*Welcoming prayer* can help. A great prayer for busy moms, we can pray it wherever we are in the midst of our big feelings. It is short, easy to memorize, and powerful. Through welcoming prayer, we obediently release our desires to Jesus, trust him to meet our deepest needs, and welcome him into the heart of our biggest struggles. Here's a version of welcoming prayer we've found incredibly powerful, adapted from *The Spiritual Disciplines Handbook* by Adele Calhoun:

*Jesus, I release my need to feel safe and secure.*
*Welcome, Jesus, welcome.*

*Jesus, I release my need to be loved and accepted.*
*Welcome, Jesus, welcome.*

*Jesus, I release my need to control this person or event.*
*Welcome, Jesus, welcome.*

*Jesus, I release my need to change reality and receive it as it is.*
*Welcome, Jesus, welcome.*

Welcoming prayer invites us to release our idols and disordered desires to Jesus, trusting that he will meet our needs better than we ever could. We welcome Jesus into our desires as they are now, no matter how disordered they may be, trusting that he will transform them. Over time, welcoming prayer gives Jesus room to gently reorder our desires, growing our ability to trust and obey him.

When learning this prayer, people often get stuck on the word *need*. Didn't Jesus say in Matthew 6 that God knows we need the security of food and clothing? Didn't God create us to need love, have agency, and work to change unjust realities? Of course, and God doesn't ask us to stop needing what we need. Instead, Jesus asks us to trust God for our needs, and when we obey him by seeking first the kingdom of God, he promises our needs will be met. Welcoming prayer opens us to the will and timing of God, which is the essence of trust and obedience: Not my will, but yours God.

> **REFLECT:** *How do you feel about the invitation to release your needs and trust God to meet them in God's way and God's timing?*

As we pray welcoming prayer over and over, even when the words stick in our throats, we slowly relinquish our demand for our versions of love, safety, and control. When desires battle within, resulting in anger and even rage, we can release those desires and then welcome Jesus into our reality: into the minivan with a tantruming child, at the kitchen table tutoring our learning-disabled teenager, in the rocking chair with the baby who just won't fall asleep. Without judging ourselves and our desires, we tell Jesus, "Well, here it is. The reality of it. And the reality of how angry I am in the midst of it. Here it is, Jesus, and I welcome you into all of it. Your will be done."

As we obediently release our desires to God, hour after hour, year after year, whenever we're triggered or angry, we will come to see that God can be trusted to meet our deepest needs.

## GOD CALLS US TO TRUST AND OBEY

As you read through the welcoming prayer, which of the stanzas is easiest or hardest for you to pray? Why?

### AN INVITATION: WELCOMING PRAYER

Not only is welcoming prayer a wonderful tool that helps us order our desires before God, it's a great in-the-moment prayer. We can pray it while changing diapers, while mediating between bickering siblings, and while facing our teen who's taken the car without permission. Memorize the prayer and pray it any time you feel yourself starting to get angry. As a shortcut, simply pray, "Welcome, Jesus, welcome."

# HERODIAS MAKES ROOM FOR
## THE DEVIL AND NEVER GETS FREE

One of our favorite spiritual directors, Fr. Richard Rohr, often says, "If you don't transform your pain, you'll transmit it." That sounds ominous, and the last thing we mothers need is another way to feel bad about ourselves. Still, there is no denying it: the pain our grandparents inflicted on our parents was often inflicted on us, and we then inflict some of that on our children.

Perhaps more damaging than our out-of-control screaming or passive-aggression is the anger we do control: the grudges we harbor and nurse like Herodias. Unable to kill John in the heat of her initial rage, Herodias nurses a grudge.

> **OBSERVE** *Mark 6:17-29: List every place Herodias's grudge shows up.*

Herodias's grudge has dire consequences and perpetuates the murderous legacy of her family:

— She entraps and exploits her daughter, who is made complicit in murder.

— She takes advantage of her husband and influences him to imprison John, and eventually to murder him.

— She murders John, God's own prophet.

— Because of her grudge, Jesus loses his cousin, and John's disciples lose their leader and have to bury his beheaded body.

Herodias's grudge poisons her as well. John may have been the one in jail, but Herodias is the one who's bound. She is chained by her own pain and anger, trapped inside her own history of trauma, and desperately clinging to her broken plan to get the love, security, and control she craves. Paul warns us in Ephesians to not sin in our anger, and follows it with practical advice: "Be angry but do not sin; do not let the sun go down on your anger, and do not make room for the devil" (Ephesians 4:26-27, NRSVUE). This is Herodias's sin. She made room for the devil by nursing her anger night after night. Having rejected all of God's invitations, she experiences no transformation, and everyone around her pays the price.

> **REFLECT:** *Sit for a moment with the truth that nursing our anger makes room for the devil to wreak destruction. This is not meant as a time of condemnation, simply a moment to reflect on the weightiness of nursing our grudges.*

Tragically, when we don't get free, we transmit our pain and bind our children. But don't lose heart. Jesus wants to break the pattern of generational trauma in our families. His grace is bigger than the biggest family sin. Rather than nursing our grudges, Jesus invites us to let go of them and let him transform our pain so we don't have to transmit it. This can involve healing prayer, spiritual direction, forgiveness, therapy, and even legal recourse. If we turn to Jesus with our pain, he will show us the right path to take and he will walk with us through the pain and anger that bind us, setting us free on the other side.

## GOD TRANSFORMS US AND SETS US FREE

1. What grudges did your parents nurse? How did that affect you?

2. What grudges do you nurse? What have you told yourself to keep your anger burning? How have your grudges affected your children?

## AN INVITATION: RELEASING YOUR GRUDGES

Take a minute to ask the Spirit to reveal any grudges you have and how they're being passed down to your kids. Ask the Spirit to free you from any anger that is keeping you bound. Write the welcoming prayer with what God raises, releasing your needs for safety, love, and control.

# Day 5

## GOD INVITES ANGRY MOTHERS
## TO BE AGENTS OF SHALOM

Let's imagine what could have happened if Herodias had been transformed by the love of God instead of nursing a grudge. God would have forgiven her and helped her heal. Over time, God would have given her the power to forgive her grandfather and other toxic family members. God could have stopped her family legacy of murder in her generation. Having made no room for the devil, Herodias could have become a speaker of truth and encouragement, marked by compassion and forgiveness. Filled with God's love, Herodias would have become a shalom-bearer.

While anger can lead to sin, it can also lead to the work of shalom. God gives the good gift of anger so that we can live in the truth—of our emotions, our relationships, and our world—and have the energy to act as God's agent of harmony and wholeness. This is what the apostle Paul wanted for the Ephesian church.

> **OBSERVE** *Ephesians 4:22-32: Paul gives a set of contrasts meant to help the Ephesian church know what it looks like to "put off your old self, which is being corrupted by its deceitful desires; to be made new in the attitude of your minds." Fill in the chart to observe those contrasts. Fill in the following chart to observe those contrasts.*

"Forgiving each other, just as in Christ God forgave you" (v. 32) may be the most important act of shalom on Paul's whole list. Forgiveness is the engine of the gospel. Jesus forgives us of all our sin and calls us to forgive those who sin against us. When we feel angry, forgiving our offenders releases the healing and shalom of God in both our lives and the lives of others.

While forgiveness releases us from bitterness and makes reconciliation possible, women, especially Christian women, often receive the message that we have to forgive quickly because feeling angry is not okay. Or that we're allowed to feel righteous anger when others are hurt, but we're selfish if we get angry when we're hurt. But Paul's writing in Ephesians 4 makes clear that feeling anger, for ourselves or others, is not the problem; harming others in the midst of our anger is the problem. Rather than judging our anger, what if we see our anger as a sign that we long for God's shalom?

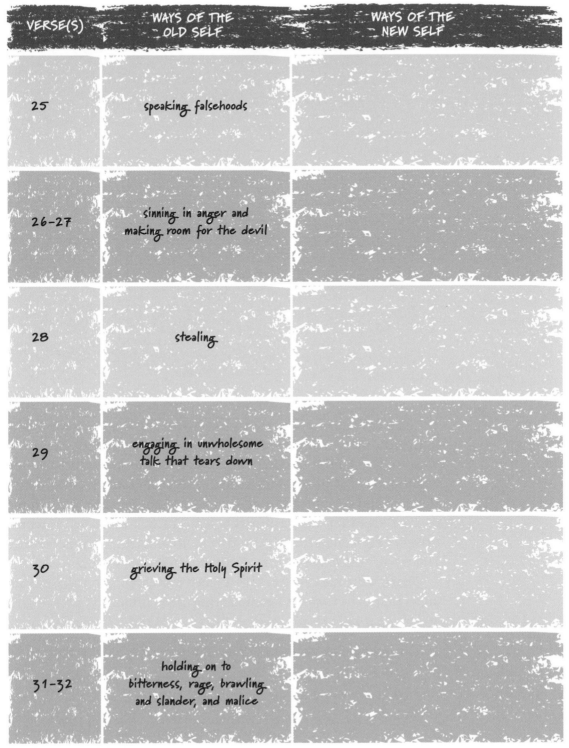

| VERSE(S) | WAYS OF THE OLD SELF | WAYS OF THE NEW SELF |
|---|---|---|
| 25 | speaking falsehoods | |
| 26-27 | sinning in anger and making room for the devil | |
| 28 | stealing | |
| 29 | engaging in unwholesome talk that tears down | |
| 30 | grieving the Holy Spirit | |
| 31-32 | holding on to bitterness, rage, brawling and slander, and malice | |

**REFLECT:** *What messages have you received about anger? In light of this study and Paul's writing to the Ephesians, what aspects of that message do you want to challenge?*

History is full of mothers who, filled with holy anger, allowed God to transform their stories of abuse and sorrow to become agents of shalom. Think of Sojourner Truth, who escaped slavery, became an abolitionist, and successfully sued a white man for her son's liberty. Her pain and anger transformed her into a force for shalom. Or think of Cary Lightner whose thirteen-year-old was killed by a drunk driver—Cary went on to found MADD, Mothers Against Drunk Driving. That's pain and anger transformed into a force for shalom.

Even if we're not called to start a social movement, God can use our anger to spur us toward shalom-bearing in important ways. We might:

 — forgive our "enemies"

 — find help for ourselves or our children if we're being abused or mistreated

 — speak up when we see injustice

 — seek forgiveness and reconciliation when we sin in anger

God gave us anger so we could light a flame that shines in the darkness, warms those who are cold, and burns away evil and injustice. When we feel hurt, our anger can spur us toward the work of forgiveness and reconciliation. When we see injustice, our anger can spur us toward defending victims or rebuilding broken systems. May God use our anger for God's shalom.

## GOD INVITES US TO BE AGENTS OF SHALOM

1. Where might God be using your anger as an invitation toward shalom? For yourself? Your family? Others?

2. What injustice in your household, workplace, or community makes you angry? How can you join someone already working on this issue?

## AN INVITATION: FORGIVENESS

Ask the Holy Spirit to reveal someone you need to forgive, then give you power to begin the forgiveness process. This may involve praying "Help me be willing to be willing to be willing . . . to forgive." Write down the prayer the Holy Spirit gives you.

*Family Sabbath*

We've created a kids' version of welcoming prayer that your whole family can pray.

*I want to feel safe.*
*Welcome, Jesus, welcome.*

*I want to feel special.*
*Welcome, Jesus, welcome.*

*I wish I were in control.*
*Welcome, Jesus, welcome.*

*I wish things were better.*
*Welcome, Jesus, welcome.*

Our children are in the early stages of identifying their emotions and sharing them with God. When our children are melting down, resisting us, or fighting with each other, their primal desires for safety, love, and agency often lie at the root of their anger. This prayer acknowledges those desires and welcomes Jesus into their experiences and feelings. Trusting Jesus to show up, we don't have to judge or talk them out of their desires.

It's okay for our children to take baby steps in what will become a lifelong journey of letting Jesus into their lives. Many of us need those baby steps as well, so pray it as a family! Welcome, Jesus, welcome.

# When We're Grasping for Control

## GROUP BIBLE STUDY

### CHECK IN ON LAST WEEK

Allow each person to take one to two minutes to share:

— How did your devotionals and family sabbath practice go last week? (No shame or guilt if you didn't get to them.)

— What did you hear (if anything) from God through the studies, the reflection questions, and the invitations?

### INTRODUCTION TO WEEK 6

Have someone read the following aloud:

Whether or not we identify with the labels "helicopter mom," "tiger mom," or "snowplow mom," most of us struggle with trying to control our children, their outcomes, and their environments. Mary, the mother of Jesus, was no helicopter mom. But as we'll learn this week, even she had to learn to release control of her son to his perfect parent, God the Father. In Luke 2, we read the only account of Jesus as a child. At twelve and on the cusp of becoming a man, he invites his mother to see him with new eyes.

### OPENING ACTIVITY

FILL IN THE BLANKS with how you have tried to control your children's destinies. We've filled in two of ours:

If I *didn't give my kids sugar their first two years of life*, they would *never crave sugar*.

If I *left my newborn in the bassinet when his older brother came to visit me in the hospital*, they would *never have sibling rivalry*.

— If I _____,

    my kid would _____

— If I _____,

    my kid would _____

— If I _____,

    my kid would _____

SHARE one of the most embarrassing things you wrote!

VIDEO

WATCH this week's video.

BIBLE STUDY

READ Luke 2:41-51 aloud.

1. In verses 41-47, answer the five "W questions": who, what, where, why, and when.

2. What thoughts and feelings do you think flooded Mary when she first realized her son was missing, then searched for three days?

3. When Mary finds Jesus in the temple in verse 48, how does she respond?

4. What does that response reveal about:

    — Her assessment of Jesus' behavior?

    — How she sees her role as a parent?

5. If you found your own child in the temple after searching for three days:

    — What emotions or thoughts would flood through you?

    — What would you say to your child?

6. In verse 49, how does Jesus respond to Mary's outcry?

    — What is he trying to tell his mother?

— What would you have said at that point if you were Mary?

7. In verses 50-51, how does Mary respond to Jesus' words?

## HOLY SPIRIT CHECK-IN

Take one minute to ask the Holy Spirit to help you fill in the blank:

*God, it would be easier to release control over my child/children if*

_____.

Go around the circle and pray,

*"God, it would be easier to release them if _____,*
*help me release them."*

## BREATH PRAYER

Take two minutes of silence to practice this breath prayer individually. Then share what, if anything, you experienced while praying. If you feel drawn to this prayer, you can pray it throughout the week.

INHALE: *I am anxiously searching*

EXHALE: *God find them*

## LEADER BENEDICTION

*Father God, our desire to protect and rescue our children is strong. And so we grasp for control, looking for ways to ensure their safety and success. We confess that too often we want to be the Holy Spirit in their lives. Help us open our clutching hands and release our children to you. Help us open our hands to receive your Spirit. Amen.*

# GOD MEETS MARY AS SHE REMEMBERS

*Day 1*

If you've ever lost a child in a store, you know the panic that grabs hold of your chest. *What if something terrible has happened to them?* Your momma bear kicks in and you're off—enlisting the help of strangers, checking under clothing racks—you will not stop until your baby's found. If you're like us, self-recrimination bombards you as you search: *What kind of mother loses her child? What will people think of me? I should have been more alert.*

Mary may feel the same terror and self-recrimination when she realizes she has lost Jesus. While searching, she may hear the lies our Accuser has whispered to mothers through the ages:

— Your child is hopelessly lost.

— It's all your fault.

— You've got to figure out how to rescue them.

The story of Passover, which Mary celebrated right before losing track of her son, counters the Accuser's lies. Passover celebrates God's incredible rescue of the Israelites from hundreds of years of slavery. It reminds us that:

— We are never hopelessly lost.

— Even when we've done everything right, there are still pharaohs, enemies intent on our destruction.

— God is our rescuer, stronger than any enemy.

> **OBSERVE** *Exodus 13:3-10: How should the Jewish people explain Passover to their children?*

By taking a week to celebrate Passover every year, the Israelites rehearsed the story of God bringing them out of slavery and taking them to their new home, a land flowing with milk and honey. They not only recited the history, but reenacted parts of it for seven days, remembering how God sustained them when they escaped from Egypt.

Why did God want them to reenact instead of merely retell? We get a clue in verse 9, where God tells them that this observance will imprint the story like a sign on their hands and a reminder on their foreheads. God met them every year through the embodied nature of this holiday, instructing them in Exodus and elsewhere in Scripture to: clear their homes of anything with yeast; eat only unleavened bread to remember how there wasn't time for their bread to rise; slaughter a lamb; and enjoy a ceremonial feast of symbolic foods. God met them and shaped them into a people who could say: *We are people God is bringing out of bondage and taking home to freedom.*

So when Mary can't find Jesus in the caravan, she isn't meeting God in God's great story of rescue for the first time. She has been meeting God in this way for more than two decades. Surely her friends and family encourage her to remember that story by reminding her, "God takes care of our children. With God's help, we'll find him."

Passover is our story too, and God meets us each time we remember it. Like Mary, many of us have had the heart-pounding experience of losing track of a child. As our kids grow older, they can feel lost in so many other ways—struggling with mental health issues, straying from their faith, pursuing a path we fear will lead to destruction. Their list of enemies also grows—social media, bullying culture, date rape drugs, school shootings, and institutions that don't protect all of our children. In all these vulnerable places, we become susceptible to our enemy, the Accuser, who tempts us to grasp for control and whispers, *"Your child is lost and doomed. You should have protected them better and need to rescue them."* When the lies of the Accuser flood our minds, we can counter them with truth: We worship a God bigger than any enemy who comes against our children. Our God specializes in rescuing the lost and doomed.

REFLECT: *What lies haunt you when your children are lost? What is God's truth?*

Like Mary, we need God's people to help us remember God's story. Just as God commanded the Jewish people to gather and remember God's rescue through the Passover, Jesus commands the church to gather and remember his great rescue through celebrating Communion. Each time we eat the bread and drink the wine, we are imprinted as people redeemed from bondage. In fact, every part of our life together as the church—Sunday morning, small groups, and our love of neighbors—reminds us of God's faithfulness.

Scripture records a miraculous encounter with an angel only once in Mary's life. But day to day, moment to moment, and in a crisis when her son went missing, God met Mary as she remembered, with her people, God's great rescue mission and never-ending faithful love. As we remember our Father's never-ending faithful love, he will meet us as surely as he met Mary.

## GOD MEETS US WHERE WE ARE

1. How do the practices of your church help you remember God's story of rescue? Perhaps it's through Bible study, liturgy, or music. (If your experience of church has been more harmful than faith-affirming, use this space to share with God your longing for a faith community that helps you remember the right story.)

2. What stories or passages in Scripture do you want to remember when your children are "lost"?

## MARY HAS AN HONEST CONVERSATION WITH JESUS

Mary loses her son for three whole days. Imagine the emotions cascading through her as she and Joseph walk as fast as they can the twenty miles back to Jerusalem. Imagine the worst-case scenarios that flood her mind as she wonders what could have happened to Jesus.

Mary and Joseph eventually find Jesus sitting among the rabbis in the temple courts, listening to them and asking them questions.

> **OBSERVE** *Luke 2:46-48: What verbs describe Jesus' actions? How do the crowds respond to Jesus? Why?*

There sits Jesus, a twelve-year-old boy in the midst of the most learned people of the land, holding his own. No wonder his parents are astonished.

But Mary doesn't respond like a proud mom who's watching her child shine. Instead, she asks, "Son, why have you treated us like this? Your father and I have been anxiously searching for you." Despite experiencing a miraculous birth and angelic prophecy that Jesus is God's Messiah, Mary is still a mother with a missing child who's been searching anxiously for three days, wondering if something horrible has happened to him. Her honest response sounds like a cry of exasperation.

> **REFLECT:** *When have you asked your child some version of the question, "Why have you treated us this way?" What feelings lie behind that question?*

Most of us can relate to Mary. Our kids' failures and disobedience, even their appropriate steps toward independence, can feel like personal attacks. We want to cry out, "Why have you treated me this way?" *Don't you know how hard I've worked to be a good mom, to give you what you need, and prepare you for the future? How dare you thwart my good plans for you?*

When we fear our children are lost, or straying from the path we charted for them, many of us relate to Mary's anxious search: *I've been anxiously searching for the right school, the right treatment, or the right way to deal with all your struggles. I wait anxiously for you to call, or text, or come home in the last minutes of curfew. I search and search and search, so afraid that if I stop, you will be permanently lost.*

Mary's honest response to Jesus models the kinds of conversations we can have with God. Jesus doesn't chastise his mother for telling him that she takes his "bad" behavior personally. He doesn't chastise us either. Instead, he invites us to tell him all our big feelings and confess the ways we over-function, playing God when really we're just terrified moms.

Like Jesus, whose next step of development means dwelling in his Father's house, our kids also belong with God. We loosen our tight grip on our children when we tell God about the control we want to have and the fear that undergirds it all. We, like Mary, can tell Jesus all about it.

## GOD WELCOMES US INTO HONEST CONVERSATION

1. What paths have you charted for your children? What fears do you have that they may get hurt, lost, or wander off your path?

2. How are you trying to ensure they stay on your path? (For example: rescuing them from consequences that would help them grow, staying up late to help them finish a project they put off, talking them to death and not praying.)

Share with Jesus what you've written, knowing you will not be chastised. Listen to hear how Jesus responds. Write down anything you hear.

## GOD CALLS MAMA EWES TO TRUST AND OBEY

*Day 3*

No one faults Mary for searching for her son. She would have been negligent if she had not gone looking. And it's hard to imagine her walking up calmly and saying with a cheerful smile, "Oh, darling, how wonderful to see you here!"

Still, in response to Mary's question—"Why have you treated us like this?"—Jesus says, "Why were you searching for me? . . . Didn't you know I had to be in my Father's house?" He seems to imply: *You misunderstand what's happening here. I don't need to be rescued. I need to do the will of the Father.* As important as Mary's parenting has been, his ultimate parent is God.

This was good news for Mary and it's good news for us. God is our children's perfect parent, the good shepherd who relentlessly searches for them when they are lost. Yet as mamas who love our lambs, we can be tempted to believe that we, not God, are the good shepherd.

In Isaiah, God reminds us that we are sheep, mama ewes in need of a shepherd:

> He tends his flock like a shepherd:
> He gathers the lambs in his arms
> and carries them close to his heart;
> **he gently leads those that have young**. (Isaiah 40:11,
>     emphasis added)

Domesticated sheep, even the mamas, can't survive without a shepherd. Mama ewes can't fight off lions or bears or wolves. They don't know where dangerous cliffs lie in the dark. Mama ewes need a shepherd. What great news that our good shepherd is gentle with us as he leads us!

> **OBSERVE** *Psalm 23: Given all that the good shepherd does, what's the role of the psalmist?*

Psalm 23 reminds us that God is the good shepherd, and we can rest in God's care. Both mama ewes and their lambs need a shepherd who goes out with them, guides them, protects them, and sets out to find them yet again when they wander off. They need a shepherd who makes them lie down when they need rest, who refreshes, protects, and blesses them. They need a shepherd whose goodness and love will relentlessly pursue them forever.

LIES VERSUS THE TRUTH

| THE ACCUSER'S LIES TO US | TRUTH WE CAN TRUST | PRACTICAL WAY TO RECEIVE |
|---|---|---|
| You are <u>not enough</u>. You don't have what your children need. | I lack nothing under the shepherd's care. | |
| You need to <u>be perfect</u>. If you're perfect, you will raise perfect children. | God is the perfect shepherd who invites me to rest. | |
| You must <u>solve all your kids' problems</u>. Keep working and solving all the time. | Our good shepherd knows and guides me along right paths. | |
| You <u>can't allow your kids to suffer</u>. You have to keep your kids from experiencing any pain. | God walks with my children even in the valley of the shadow of death. | |
| You need to be a <u>mama-bear</u>. You alone have to protect your kids at all costs. | God's rod and staff protect my children, feeding them in the presence of enemies. | |
| You have to be <u>all-loving</u>. Your love must be all-encompassing and never-ending. | God's goodness and mercy relentlessly pursue my children forever. | |

In response to our good shepherd, we mama ewes need only to receive. When the Accuser tempts us to believe that it is our job to be the shepherd, we can rebuke him by receiving the true shepherd's provision, rest, guidance, companionship, protection, goodness, and mercy. Hallelujah!

## GOD CALLS US TO TRUST AND OBEY

How does God's invitation to be a mama ewe rather than a shepherd feel to you?

### AN INVITATION: RECEIVING FROM THE GOOD SHEPHERD

Looking over the Lies Versus the Truth table again, choose one way you want to receive from the shepherd today. Then try this breath prayer:

INHALE: *You are my shepherd.*

EXHALE: *I receive your* _____.
(Fill in the blank with what you want to receive from the shepherd today: *provision, rest, guidance, companionship, protection, goodness,* or *mercy.*)

## Day 4

## GOD TRANSFORMS MARY AND SETS HER FREE

Mary is a model of faithfulness, but that doesn't mean she never struggles to release her grasp on Jesus. In Mark 3, for example, thinking Jesus is out of his mind, Mary and Jesus' brothers go to take charge of him and bring him home. But Jesus won't go with them and instead declares to the crowds, "Who are my mother and my brothers? . . . Here are my mother and my brothers! Whoever does God's will is my brother and sister and mother" (vv. 33-35).

Talk about a hard way to receive your child's claim of independence! Most of the time, though, Mary isn't tempted to grasp for control. Instead, she ponders and treasures God's words and work in her son. Luke records four instances where Mary responds to surprising revelation.

**OBSERVE:** *In each passage, how does Mary respond to surprising or difficult to understand pronouncements?*

*Luke 1:28-29*

*Luke 2:19*

*Luke 2:25-33*

*Luke 2:49-51*

Mary could have received the prophecies from Gabriel, the shepherds, and Simeon and concluded that she needed to make it all happen, that she needed to ensure her son would fulfill his destiny. After her experience of losing Jesus in Jerusalem, Mary could have clamped down on him and his ability to roam freely. But her response, rather than quashing or controlling, is to treasure all these things in her heart.

> **REFLECT:** *Luke 2:50 says that Mary and Joseph didn't understand what Jesus said. How can we treasure what we don't understand as Mary did in verse 51?*

Instead of trying to figure out what God wants her to do, Mary receives God's invitation to be. Mary models the transforming freedom of pondering over planning, of treasuring over doing. She spends decades treasuring what were only minutes of revelation. This is not passive resignation, but rather an embracing of the freedom to be still and release control while God reveals the plan for her son.

When our children are lost in one way or another, releasing control and pondering what God is up to may not feel like freedom. It may feel like being handcuffed. But when our children are lost, freedom means releasing them into God's hands and treasuring the small glimpses we see of God working in their lives. When we ponder and treasure, we experience freedom from the grim demand that we be all knowing, loving, powerful, and present.

As Mary spends decades remembering, pondering, and treasuring, God transforms and frees her, not to be a better mother, but a beloved daughter who can trust her Father to take care of her child.

## GOD TRANSFORMS US AND SETS US FREE

1. What have you noticed about your child, or have others said about your child, that you wonder about, ponder, or treasure?

2. How have you seen traces of transformation and freedom in your own parenting? How has God been preparing you to release your children more fully?

**AN INVITATION: RELEASING AND RECEIVING PRAYER**

Begin with your palms down, resting in your lap. Turn over to God everything you tightly grasp onto for your children. Then flip your hands up to receive from God, and say, "I receive what you wish to give." Repeat this cycle of releasing and receiving for as long as you wish.

*Day 5*

## GOD INVITES MARY TO BE AN AGENT OF SHALOM

If any mother was called to be an agent of shalom, it was Mary. With each step of faithfulness, Mary released her son into his ministry of shalom. But at the foot of the cross, God invites Mary into the most stunningly difficult act of shalom-bearing thus far—to stay present with her son as he suffers and dies, to stay present when there's nothing she can do or control. Mary's vigil by her son's cross has much to teach us.

**OBSERVE** *John 19:25-34: In verse 25, what are Mary and the other women doing? List everything Mary witnessed in verses 26-34.*

Mary stands at the foot of the cross, watching her son as he's tortured and slowly dying. With nothing left to do or fix, Mary stands with Jesus through every excruciating minute.

Watching your child suffer can feel unbearable. In our experience, nothing illuminates our desire to control more than the inability to prevent or ease our own child's suffering. But God invites us to stand with our children instead of in front of them slaying the dragons headed their way. Rather than giving advice, fretting, or attempting to control where they go, who they see, and what they do, we are invited to stand with them as they live out their own journeys with God, even when those journeys take them through the valley of the shadow of death.

The shadow of death stalks us all. Our children, our friends, our neighbors, and our brothers and sisters around the world all suffer greatly at times. We can't fix much for any of them. But we can stand in solidarity with them without looking away.

REFLECT: *How difficult is it for you to stand with the suffering when you are unable to fix the problem?*

When we stand in solidarity with those who suffer, even though there may be nothing concrete we can do to help their problems, we give the gift of loving presence. We embody our loving Father, who never turns his gaze from our suffering. When we show up, withhold our advice and agendas, weep with the weeping, and link arms with the suffering, we bear the balm of shalom. May God give us the endurance to stand with those who suffer.

## GOD INVITES US TO BE AGENTS OF SHALOM

1. Think of the last time one of your children was suffering. How did you respond? Swooping in and solving? Standing with them? Some other way?

2. Who inside or outside your family is suffering right now? What might it look like to stand with them?

## AN INVITATION: SITTING IN SOLIDARITY

One of the reasons we don't want to look at the suffering of others is because we think it will overwhelm us—with sadness, guilt, or a sense of impotence.

Ask the Holy Spirit to bring to mind someone or some group who suffers. Picture Jesus tucking that person or group into his heart. Sit in solidarity with them for two minutes. As you finish up, ask the Spirit to remind you throughout the day that this person or group is tucked safely away in the heart of God.

One of the ways that we try to "rescue" our children is by bombarding them with advice and criticism. Sometimes we are so desperate to be useful, or so afraid that without our constant attention our children will suffer, that we crowd out their ability to hear from God directly.

To practice humbly releasing each other into the care of God, announce that this week you will have an "advice-free sabbath." Explain that while it's important to help each other grow in godliness, God has sent the Holy Spirit to teach us, lead us, and show us when we are off the path. We cannot be one another's Holy Spirit. Today, we will reinforce this truth by refraining from criticizing anyone or giving any advice.

*Family Sabbath*

Some helpful tips:

1. Make a funny hand motion people can use if someone accidentally starts to criticize or give advice. It could be a wiggle of the nose or a tug on the ear, for example.

2. When you are tempted to give advice, say to yourself, "Look at my sweet child, who is _____. I wonder what God's plan is for that."

At the end of the day, share what it was like to withhold criticism and advice. Share what it was like to not receive criticism and advice. Pray that God would release everyone in the family from feeling like they can or should be anyone else's Holy Spirit.

# When Our Hearts Are Breaking

## GROUP BIBLE STUDY

### CHECK IN ON LAST WEEK

Allow each person to take one to two minutes to share:

— How did your devotionals and family sabbath practice go last week? (No shame or guilt if you didn't get to them.)

— What did you hear (if anything) from God through the studies, the reflection questions, and the invitations?

### INTRODUCTION TO WEEK 7

Have someone read the following aloud:

We call it heartbreak because we feel it in our bodies. We feel the pain, sorrow, and devastation in our chests, our throats, and our guts. When we face infidelity, addiction, divorce, mental illness, or death, when we or those we love have been victimized, scarred by tragedy, or caught in a vortex of sin, our hearts can feel like they're actually shattering.

In our final chapter, we return to Hagar, whose heart is breaking. In week one, we learned how Hagar, a fleeing mother-to-be, met El Roi, the God who sees her. Seventeen years later, she finds herself in the desert once more but this time with her son Ishmael walking beside her. Out of water and out of options, they are dying from thirst. And Hagar is heartbroken.

### OPENING ACTIVITY

**THINK** of an experience where your heart was breaking. Without telling the story of what broke your heart, share a sentence about what that experience felt like in your body.

### VIDEO

**WATCH** this week's video.

## BIBLE STUDY

READ Genesis 21:5-21 aloud.

1. Fill out the following table, noticing similarities and differences between Genesis 16 and Genesis 21.

2. Put yourself in Hagar's sandals this second time in the desert.

   — What emotions do you experience? How do those emotions compare to the last time you were in the desert, pregnant with Ishmael?

   — How do you feel when God meets you?

| COMPARE AND CONTRAST | GENESIS 16 | GENESIS 21 |
|---|---|---|
| Circumstances leading up to Hagar finding herself in the desert | **Verses 1-6**<br>• Hagar is forced to have sex and carry Abram's child<br>• Hagar despises Sarai<br>• Sarai blames Hagar for her pain.<br>• With Abram's blessing, Sarai mistreats Hagar<br>• Abram and Sarai never call Hagar by name<br>• Hagar leaves of her own volition | **Verses 8-14** |
| The initial encounter between Hagar and the angel | **Verses 7-8**<br>• She's pregnant and alone in the desert<br>• She's near a spring<br>• God finds her<br>• God asks her two questions: where have you come from, where are you going<br>• She answers the questions | **Verses 14-17** |
| The continuing conversation between Hagar and the angel | **Verses 9-13**<br>• The angel tells Hagar to go back to her mistress and submit<br>• He gives her promises about her future:<br>  — She'll give birth<br>  — His name will be Ishmael because God has heard her misery<br>  — He will be wild (free)<br>  — He will live in hostility toward his brothers<br>• Hagar names the Lord "El Roi," you are the God who sees me | **Verses 17-18** |
| Where do we see transformation? | **Verses 14-16**<br>• Hundreds of years later, the well is still called Beer Lahai Roi, in honor of Hagar's meeting with God<br>• Instead of dying in the desert, Hagar lives and has a son<br>• Abram listens to Hagar's story and gives the boy the name that the angel gave Hagar | **Verses 19-21** |

3. How would you summarize the main differences between the two stories?

4. How does the transformation we see in 21:19-21 fulfill some of the promises God made to Hagar in chapter 16?

## HOLY SPIRIT CHECK-IN

Take two minutes to present to the Holy Spirit any places where you feel heartbroken, hopeless, weary, or isolated. Listen for anything the Spirit says in reply. Briefly share what you experienced.

## BREATH PRAYER

Take two minutes of silence to practice this breath prayer individually. Then share what, if anything, you experienced while praying. If you feel drawn to this prayer, you can pray it throughout the week. (Note: If you are currently experiencing heartbreak, you may not have words for prayer. If so, perhaps you can sit still and simply breathe. Each inhalation and exhalation is a prayer, and our God in heaven receives each one as a precious gift.)

INHALE: *When I cannot watch*

EXHALE: *You are the God who sees*

*Father, Son, and Holy Spirit, thank you that when our hearts are broken, your heart breaks as well. You know the depths of our sorrow. You know how we feel abandoned at times. You know we lose hope. We confess that we grow weary. Give us eyes to see you, ears to hear you, and the strength to endure. Draw near to us, merciful God, in our time of trouble. Amen.*

## GOD MEETS HAGAR WHERE SHE IS

*Day 1*

Hagar faces perhaps the most excruciating experience for any mother—the impending death of her child. We don't know what Abraham said to Hagar as he put a skin of water on her shoulders and handed her some food before sending them off. Maybe he tried to console her, pointing out that she would no longer be enslaved. Maybe he told her about the promise God had given him, that Ishmael's descendants would become a great nation.

Whatever he did, it wasn't enough.

God tells Abraham to listen to Sarah, but doesn't say, "Give Hagar and Ishmael just enough food and water to survive a short while in the desert." Abraham could have sent them off with camels and servants and provisions enough to build a new life. But no. He sends them off with only the food and water that Hagar can carry, so little that in no time at all, they're out. Out of family. Out of water. Out of hope.

> **OBSERVE** *Genesis 21:15-16: What does Hagar say when she realizes they are going to die in the desert?*

Hagar, deep in the throes of grief, does the unimaginable; she walks away. She doesn't frantically try to find a well or cry out to God. She doesn't even comfort Ishmael. She gives up. She leaves Ishmael under a bush, walks fifty yards away, sits down, weeps, and waits for her son to die. In the distance, she hears Ishmael crying. He has much to cry about: his teasing of Isaac has resulted in their banishment; his father who has raised him since birth has cast him out with only the water and food his mother can carry; and he and his mother are about to die.

| **OBSERVE** *Genesis 21:17: Describe God's actions.*

In her first encounter with God, Hagar learned that God is El Roi, the one who sees her. God told Hagar to name her son "God hears" to remember how God heard her cries of misery. As she raised Ishmael, each time she called his name, she was invited to rehearse God's character as one who hears every cry in her heart. Now, in her moment of deepest anguish, she learns that God hears not only *her* cries of misery but the cries of *her child* as well. God fulfills the promise of Ishmael's name and hears Ishmael's cries.

We don't have to beg, cajole, or manipulate God to listen to our cries or the cries of our children. God hears those cries and meets all of us wherever we are.

### GOD MEETS US WHERE WE ARE

1. Where have you experienced heartbreak in your life? When have you wanted, like Hagar, to walk away?

2. Where have you, like Hagar, experienced heartbreak for your child?

**AN INVITATION: HOLY SPIRIT PAUSE**

Invite the Holy Spirit to show you how God is present with you and your child today. Write down what you hear.

## GOD WELCOMES HAGAR INTO HONEST CONVERSATION

God hears Ishmael crying and calls out, "What is the matter, Hagar?" God already knows all about the injustice and sorrow that she and Ishmael have experienced. God sees their defeated bodies, Ishmael crying and lying under a bush, Hagar sobbing a bowshot away. God feels the dryness in their mouths and hears the anguish in their weeping. God knows yet asks anyway, "What is the matter?" With this tender question, God invites Hagar, yet again, into honest conversation.

Unlike Hagar's experience seventeen years earlier, where God waited for and received her answers, here she does not reply, and God does not wait for her answer before moving the conversation forward. It's as though God knows that Hagar is too weary to answer. Instead, her salty tears are her answer. The weeping of her son is her answer. Weeping is the only answer required.

Scripture confirms that God hears our weeping as prayer. In Psalm 39:12, David cries out to God, "Do not be deaf to my weeping." And in Psalm 56:8 (NASB), David writes:

> You have taken account of my miseries;
> Put my tears in Your bottle.
> Are they not in Your book?

David is confident that God not only hears our weeping, but that God keeps a record of our tears.

Paul's letter to the Romans in chapter 8 includes imagery of wordless prayer.

**OBSERVE** *Romans 8:22-26: Notice everyone who is groaning.*

Even with the expectant hope of a new creation on the horizon, our current reality is so broken it necessitates prayer in the form of wordless groaning.

Perhaps it's not surprising that all of creation is groaning. A quick look around and evidence of creation's fall abounds. We may not even be surprised that believers are groaning as we await the final redemption of our bodies. We are, after all, people who live in the now and not yet: the kingdom is here now but not yet in its fullness; suffering and death are not yet fully vanquished. But have you ever meditated on how the Holy Spirit not only intercedes on our behalf, but intercedes with wordless groans? If the Holy Spirit, who has perfect hope for the future, can pray in groans, so can we.

> **REFLECT:** *Have you ever prayed with weeping or wordless groans? What was that like? If you haven't prayed with weeping or groans, how do you feel knowing that the Holy Spirit is interceding in this way for you?*

Hagar's experience doesn't demand that we pray with our tears or our groans, but it does give us permission to do so when that's all we've got. When our pain and anguish are so deep we don't know what to pray, when the entirety of our prayer is an inarticulate groan or snotty mess of weeping, that's the honest communication God wants to receive from us.

## GOD WELCOMES US INTO HONEST CONVERSATION

"What is the matter?" If you have the energy, answer God's question, and begin a conversation. If you don't have the energy, sit where you are, as you are, and let your tears, your groans, or even your silence be your honest communication with God.

### AN INVITATION: LAMENT

Heartbreak is exhausting. If that's where you are right now, imagine God inviting you to sit and cry, and then let your body assume the posture of your heartbreak. Groan, weep, lie down on the floor, or bury yourself in blankets.

If you have more energy, you might lament. Lament is a way God gave us to tell the truth about our pain. In fact, two-thirds of the Psalms are complaints and laments. Ask the Holy Spirit to help you lament all that is breaking your heart. If you need words, consider Psalm 6 to guide your lament. Write your lament below.

## GOD CALLS HAGAR
## TO TRUST AND OBEY

*Day 3*

After asking Hagar "What is the matter?" God instructs her not to fear and to go to Ishmael and take him by the hand.

> **OBSERVE** *Genesis 21:17-18: What reasons does God give Hagar to trust and obey these difficult instructions?*

Seventeen years ago, God told Hagar that her descendants would be too numerous to count. Here God reminds her of this promise and calls her to trust that God will fulfill it.

Before Hagar can even respond, God gives her a miracle—opening her eyes to a well of water. Did God miraculously create a well right where she needed one? Or was the well there all along and Hagar and Ishmael couldn't see it? Either way, her eyes needed to be opened; she couldn't see any hope. And then, miraculously, she could. El Roi, the God who sees, now enables Hagar to see.

In God's response to Hagar's greatest moment of anguish, God doesn't explain why they're suffering, condemn her for leaving her son alone, or chastise her for not having enough faith. God doesn't even command her to open her eyes. Instead, God opens her eyes for her. There's almost nothing Hagar must do.

Previous studies illustrated that our trust and obedience often put us in a position for God to transform us. In this story, though, Hagar's transformation requires nothing more than her tears and God's love. That's because God is bigger than any flowchart we might draw. God's love transcends our tidy rules. When Hagar can't bear to face her son's death, God meets her. When she doesn't answer God's question—*What is the matter?*—God receives her tears as her answer. When she's lost all hope for her son and can't even move, God opens her eyes.

One way to think about Hagar's experience of heartbreak is with the Ignatian concepts of *consolation* and *desolation*. Saint Ignatius used the term *desolation* to describe experiences where God feels absent. While we may believe with our minds that God is always present and working, in desolation we cannot see or feel the hand of God. In moments of desolation, we may feel abandoned by God: "My God, my God, why have you forsaken me?" (Psalm 22:1). In contrast, *consolation* refers to the experience of God drawing near, opening our eyes to see God's presence and provision. Moments of consolation encourage us, strengthen our faith, and leave us with deep gratitude— even when circumstances break our hearts.

Consolation does not always mean happiness and desolation does not always mean sorrow. God may feel inexplicably distant during times of happiness or powerfully comforting during times of sorrow. We discern the difference not by our emotions alone, but by our ability to experience the love, mercy, and grace of God in the midst of our circumstances.

Hagar experiences desolation in the desert not because God is absent, but because she can't see God. She experiences consolation as God draws near, speaks with her, and opens her eyes to see the well that will sustain her and her son. Hagar doesn't need to find a well. She doesn't need to dig a well. She needs only to receive the well that God opens her eyes to see.

> **REFLECT:** *When has God opened your eyes to a "well" when you couldn't see one? How did you receive it?*

When we are weary from heartbreak, trusting and obeying look like receiving God's consolation, receiving the wells that God opens our eyes to see. Sometimes those wells take the form of a peace that passes all understanding (Philippians 4:7), the comforting presence of God in the midst of the shadow of death (Psalm 23:4). Other times, the wells God provides take the form of friends—friends praying with us, cooking for us, taking a kid for a playdate, or stopping by to clean the bathroom. If you are in the midst of heartbreak and someone shows up offering any of those, open your door and receive God's consolation.

## GOD CALLS US TO TRUST AND OBEY

1. Where does it seem like God is absent in your child's life? How do you long for God to show up for your child?

2. How are you being invited to receive today? Through graciously accepting a meal or offer to babysit? Or maybe the Holy Spirit wants to hold you while you weep.

## AN INVITATION: EXAMEN

Ignatius of Loyola created the spiritual discipline of *examen*, where we reflect on our days and note the places of consolation, where we met God or saw God's hand, and desolation, where our eyes could not perceive the presence or provision of God. There are many ways to practice examen. We suggest spending anywhere from five to thirty minutes writing down answers to the following questions:

— *Review the day:* What events, details, conversations, and feelings did I experience today? What did I experience in my body? What occupied my mind today?

— *Reflect on the desolations and consolations of the day*: Where was it difficult to see God? What distracted me or drew me away from God? Where did I see God? What led me closer to God? What unexpected "wells" showed up?

# GOD TRANSFORMS HAGAR
# AND SETS HER FREE

When God opens Hagar's eyes, her hope is restored and she is free to trust that God's offer will hold. She fills her skin with water and gives her son a drink. She still can't see the end of the story or how it will all work out. But in the presence of God and with enough water for this moment, her heartbreak gives way to hope.

And then Hagar and Ishmael's circumstances are transformed as well.

> **OBSERVE** *Genesis 21:19-21 and 25:7-18: What happens in Hagar and Ishmael's lives after God's rescue in the barren desert? Note any evidence of transformation and freedom.*

At last, all of God's promises to Hagar from Genesis 16 are fulfilled.

When our hearts are breaking, a flourishing future may not seem like a realistic possibility. After all, suffering is never far from any of us. We, the authors, have spent sleepless, anguished nights worrying about our own children's journeys. We felt impotent and hopeless when they suffered or made dangerous choices. And we've walked together with dear friends through heartbreak as children's faith crumbled, marriages disintegrated, addiction seemed to win the day, and failed cancer treatments meant preparing young children for the death of their mother. Yet through the most barren of deserts, God consistently showed up. Sometimes we could sense the ineffable presence of God. More often though, we experienced God through the hands and feet of Christ's body, the church.

While God did not always provide the wells we desperately wanted, God always opened our eyes to see some well—a wise counselor, a shoulder to cry on, friends praying for us when our hearts were too broken to pray ourselves. God's presence and provision quenched our souls and, over time, transformed us both in profound ways.

For Tara, I have come to expect a well when one is not obvious. I used to flirt with apostasy each time something horrific happened, vacillating between yelling at God and atheism. When my daughter moved in with us after her mother died and her dad was unable to care for her, I asked her how she could still believe in God. She said, "When I was born, my dad asked God to take care of me in all the ways he couldn't. I've always known that God was with me, taking care of me." She expects God to show her wells and God has always come through. Her witness, the witness of countless friends, and my own experience of God's presence during suffering trained my eyes to look for wells. Instead of declaring God must be dead when something horrific happens, I now ask, "Where are you?" To me, this transformation feels nothing short of miraculous.

For Kathy, God opened my eyes to see both myself and God better, giving me hope in what felt like the barren desert of motherhood. During my fourteen-year "dark night of the soul," motherhood brought out the very worst of me. Despite seeing a spiritual director, going up for inner healing prayer every Sunday, and regularly confessing my sins to my husband and friends, I still felt heartbroken by my sin and feared I was permanently damaging my kids. God used Tara to open my eyes. One day, as she listened to my usual litany of self-flagellation, Tara said, "Yes . . . along with your many strengths." Strengths? I couldn't identify any strengths. So in fear and trembling, I asked God to show them to me. God gave me a list of thirty-eight strengths! That experience, the fruit of years and years of seeking God, transformed me to live in the truth that I have both strength and weakness, and that God's love and grace abound in the midst of it all.

> **REFLECT:** *How have you experienced transformation in times of heartbreak?*

There are times we moms feel deeply heartbroken. Desolation stalks and we've given up hope that God will ever show up. We wait for who or what we most love to die. In those times, Hagar's story can guide us. When we can't see God, El Roi keeps seeing us. When we can only groan or weep, the God who hears the cries of our misery listens. And in the midst of all that heartbreak, Jesus, the source of living water, comes to dwell with us and gives a drink that sets us free to hope again.

## GOD TRANSFORMS US AND SETS US FREE

As you approach the end of this seven-week Bible study, how have you experienced transformation, even if small? How has God's transcendent love blessed you and set you free?

## AN INVITATION: BEING GENTLE WITH YOURSELF

When heartbreak wipes us out, our gentle Father God invites us to be gentle with ourselves and to help others be gentle with us as well. Some suggestions:

— take a nap

— resign from some of your commitments

— move slowly, talk softly, and drive carefully

— invite others to treat you gently by sharing that you are struggling

Ask the Father how he is inviting you to be gentle with yourself today. Write down what you hear.

# Day 5

## GOD INVITES HAGAR
## TO BE AN AGENT OF SHALOM

Hagar and Ishmael's experience of God's shalom is incomplete. God predicts and Scripture confirms that Ishmael's descendants will live in hostility with their brothers. The rupture of Ishmael being kicked out of the family passes from generation to generation to generation. Even today, the Arab descendants of Ishmael and the Jewish descendants of Isaac live in conflict.

Yet after her transformational encounters with God, Hagar's legacy as a shalom-bearer is clear. We know from chapter 21 that Ishmael continues in relationship with God, that Hagar and Ishmael make a life for themselves, and that Ishmael does indeed father a great nation.

Decades later there are even more signs of God's shalom.

> **OBSERVE** *Genesis 25:7-11: What do you notice about Abraham's death and burial?*

Somehow, seventy-two years after being banished from his family, Ishmael still has a relationship with his father. He and his brother Isaac are close enough to perform a final act of love together. Because of Hagar's faithfulness, Ishmael and Isaac experience *a little more shalom.*

How do we benefit from Hagar's faithfulness? Verse 11 tells us that Isaac settles near Beer Lahai Roi, the well where Hagar met God. Hagar's story of meeting El Roi at that well became so renowned that the well was named in honor of her experience and was still called that years later when the author of Genesis penned those words. Hagar's experience of transformation shaped one tiny family during her lifetime, but her experience with El Roi, "the Living One who sees me," continues to shape our understanding of God today.

> **REFLECT:** *What do you think Hagar would have imagined her legacy to be? What might she think if she read her story with us today?*

These studies began with the assertion that God wants to lead us on a journey of spiritual transformation. As we bring our leaky buckets to Beer Lahai Roi and drink from God's living water, we can then offer this same water to a world thirsty for harmony, wholeness, and peace. We end these studies with a prayer, offered in faith, a faith born by walking through motherhood with the Living One Who Sees Us.

*May you, together with other mothers, drink deeply from the well of Living Water as you walk the path of spiritual transformation with God. May you be a light for your children, friends, and communities so they can find their way to the One who sees, hears, and gives us life.*

## GOD INVITES US TO BE AGENTS OF SHALOM

Who are the people who have been bearers of shalom when you felt alone or heartbroken? How did God use them to help you drink from Beer Lahai Roi?

### AN INVITATION: HOLY SPIRIT PAUSE

Ask the Holy Spirit to give you a small glimpse of your legacy, to show you the seeds of shalom you are planting for generations to come. Write down anything you hear.

*Family Sabbath*

A great way to teach your kids the practice of examen is the "Thank you. Sorry. Please." prayer. This prayer practice was the most common type of prayer both Kathy's and Tara's families used as the kids grew up. Each family member prays, filling in the blanks:

*Thank you for* _____.

*I'm sorry for* _____.

*Please* _____.

While this prayer doesn't use the words of examen, *consolation* and *desolation*, it trains our children to stop and reflect on their day, noticing where they're grateful to God and where they need God. For years, Kathy's son prayed every night, "Thank you for a good day. I'm sorry for not listening. Please help me have a good day tomorrow." Tara's son thanked God every night for whatever his eye landed on at the moment (lamps, Thomas trains, etc.) and then asked for more of the same. Despite feeling tempted to correct their prayers, we refrained, wanting them to go to God with whatever was in their little hearts.

But there were other times, especially as they got older, that our kids would pray specifically, aware of God's goodness and longing to see more of it. However your children engage with this discipline, you can model genuine gratitude, confession, and supplication.

*Thank you. Sorry. Please.* A simple, but powerful way for your whole family to draw nearer to God, who is waiting for all of you at the well of living water.

# A NEW BIBLE STUDY EXPERIENCE FROM INTERVARSITY PRESS

These Bible studies offer you a fresh opportunity to engage with Scripture. Each study includes:

- weekly sessions for a group of any size
- access to weekly teaching videos
- five days of individual study and reflection each week

The refreshing, accessible, and insightful content from trusted Bible teachers will encourage you in your faith!

With guidance from trusted Bible teachers, this new collection of Bible studies invites groups and individuals to take a closer look at Scripture and offers practices that create space for prayer and worship, lament, and wonder. Each six to eight week study explores Scripture through a thematic lens, beginning each week with a group session that includes both video teaching and discussion questions, followed by five days of individual study and reflection.

BRINGING THE BIBLE TO LIFE